dream homes

100 inspirational interiors

dream homes
100 inspirational interiors

Andreas von Einsiedel

Johanna Thornycroft

MERRELL
LONDON · NEW YORK

For Evelyn

contents

cool minimalism   56–66

country   67–90

opulent   91–100

Dream Homes presents a broad and stunning selection of interiors from around the world, each being, for its owner, the perfect environment in which to live. The work of many interior designers is represented, both by their own homes and in their work for clients, but also featured are homes that have been transformed simply through the vision of their talented and committed owners. The photographs throughout this book are testament to each home-owner's belief that the interpretation of their dream has come close to perfection.

Traditional or vernacular architecture and design endures, partly because in most countries it still forms the bulk of the housing stock. Completely open-plan loft-style living has ultimately suited few people, human comfort demanding certain boundaries, albeit ones that are moveable or transparent. The kitchen and, increasingly, the dining-room are no longer separate or segregated rooms, except where planning restrictions or other hazards intervene. In all but the grandest houses the dining-room tends to be multi-functional, serving also as a library, home office or occasional guest accommodation. As land becomes scarce and planning restrictions become ever tighter, the building of new homes is increasingly difficult. Instead, the current focus is on reorientation. Houses and apartments are turned back to front, halls merge with other rooms to avoid wasting space, bedrooms are given less priority than living space and state-of-the-art technology is married to the concept of old-fashioned comfort. Of course, if a dream home happens to be in the Caribbean, Africa or the Mediterranean, the approach may be slightly different – but not entirely so.

Maximizing and controlling light in new ways, even where it is plentiful, is the modern mantra governing interior design. The affordable manufacture of plate glass in the nineteenth century meant that windows could be enlarged; from the 1920s Modernism exploited this new freedom with glass in radical ways, a trend that continues as technical innovation moves forward. The most popular materials for building in the twenty-first century are those that are natural, recyclable and age well. Increasingly, relaxed social attitudes and enormous improvements in insulation and heating mean that our windows are now more likely to be left unadorned, as are ceilings and walls. Where privacy is required, blinds, filmy fabrics or opaque glass allow the maximum amount of that most precious commodity, daylight, to penetrate our interiors.

It is impossible to ignore the dictates of fashion, but a number of requirements appear to be indispensable in the dream home: it must be human in scale, comfortable in every area and stimulating to the senses. A house without books and some sort of individual adornment or clue to the owner's personality and interests is rarely an entirely successful environment. But any manner of dream home, even an empty white space, is still a powerful statement of individuality, if not always pleasing to every visitor. In this book two houses in particular stand out for their unbridled use of pattern and colour. Both are owned by women who are ceramicists based in Britain, and their interior decoration is linked inextricably to their work. On the whole, men tend to prefer more neutral colours and less pattern, relying instead on shape, texture and hard surfaces, but as women become increasingly influential in the architectural arena they, too, propound what has traditionally been a masculine aesthetic. What is also evident in this choice of one hundred dream homes is an increased awareness of the lack of rules governing 'good taste' as owners and designers alike mix, as never before, all manner of period and contemporary furniture, pictures, carpets or bibelots. This relaxation and confidence produces some fascinating interiors.

Apart from the pleasure of individual expression in the choice of stainless-steel kitchen or marble wet-room, and the pure decorative elements of a fresco or painted or papered wall panels, a dream home can be a demanding place. Heating and energy supplies are challenging issues. Communications, from sensor lighting to fire prevention, and computerized systems governing everything from re-stocking the refrigerator to the opening and closing of doors are de rigueur. A dream home is often made long before a paint colour or a sofa is chosen. In fact, technology is becoming a style statement in itself, and the owners of today may boast of inconspicuous efficiency and sustainability over fine furniture or pictures. These details are less

photogenic, of course, but represent a cost factor that will, in some cases, override the decoration budget.

In the mid-1980s, the *World of Interiors* magazine invited a group of architects to submit sketches for their dream schemes. The range of material was so diverse as to fly in the face of any known prevailing architectural fashion, and so it continues with interior design, or in some cases lack of design, as homes evolve according to function. Diversity is the spice of life and where else can you display eccentricity, showcase a prototype, impress or shock friends, or just live out a fantasy, except at home? No two homes are the same, although we all may draw on similar sources, cutting out images from magazines, collecting samples, obsessing over new products, and visiting fairs and exhibitions for inspiration. People choose a designer, sometimes subconsciously, because they believe he or she works in a particular style, but the final result will always be unique: size, layout, light, location and individual requirements dictate the outcome.

Contemporary interiors may have moved a long way from the simple shelter but few of us like a living-room without the primitive comfort of a fireplace. Even if it is a slit in the wall filled with pebbles and a flickering gas flame, it is still the basic focal point around which we arrange our living-rooms. Fitted carpets, chintz and chandeliers may come and go but a successful home is one that fulfils its owners need for comfort in a curiously international way. The dream homes that follow have been selected not only for their sheer quality and integrity, but also for their variety in terms of building type, style and location. From the outset it was our aim to offer the reader as few distractions as possible from the sheer enjoyment of 'walking' around the homes we have chosen to illustrate, so words and explanations have been kept to a minimum – just enough, in fact, to set each home in some sort of context, and to offer some hints as to how the 'look' has been so successfully achieved. If this book gives you ideas for your own home, and helps to turn your own dreams for it into a reality, our hopes will have been fulfilled.

classic contemporary 1–27

1 Maximum impact

An international fashion and homeware designer collaborated with a top interior designer to create an exceptionally desirable apartment for himself near London's Hyde Park. As only one bedroom was required, the existing space was reorganized to maximize the living and entertaining areas, each room almost floodlit by the enormous original windows. Built for a banking grandee in the 1860s, it was bought, newly decorated, from a developer in the 1990s. It is rare to find such balanced space and volume in London apartments, except where a lateral conversion has been carried out. Everything was replaced, apart from the magnificent windows, surviving panelling and mouldings, and a pair of floor-to-ceiling mirrors in what was originally the ballroom. Reclaimed oak floorboards were laid throughout, creating a neutral ground for the almost entirely white interior. Owner and designer both realized early on in the project that scale was to be the dominant factor – the ceiling and window heights would dwarf conventional furniture and antiques – so virtually everything would be designed and made specially for the apartment. Luxurious understatement created by fine workmanship and materials sums up this much-admired interior.

classic contemporary

classic contemporary

2 Architectural attention

In a bid to restore some of the missing nineteenth-century decorative detail in this large west London house the owner looked to Paris for inspiration. Formerly let as individual rooms, the house was eventually granted planning permission to be reconverted into a single-family dwelling. A daunting amount of work had to be undertaken but the owner praises her architect for his continuous attention to detail and meticulous planning in creating a gem of a family home. So little survived from the original that the owner decided to re-create the drawing-room in the style of a 14th arrondissement salon by adding mouldings, a mirror surround, French windows and a Louis XV chimney-piece. The floors were laid with new, specially finished parquet, giving the room a chic Parisian look. Within this pure-white space are set a large Bridget Riley painting, an orange leather Mies van der Rohe day-bed and a charcoal portrait by Alison Lambert. The lamp is by Arco and the rug is from David Gill. The pale-green kitchen has basalt work surfaces, while the bedroom gleams with silver leaf and a mirrored screen designed by Syrie Maugham.

classic contemporary

classic contemporary

3 Master class

This apartment spans the raised ground floor of two elegant houses in London. It is entered through a square hall, devoid of any decoration or furniture. This taupe-coloured space is lit both artificially and by diffused light from the rooms on either side. The door straight ahead leads to the designer–owner's large bedroom; to the right is the pure-white Siematic kitchen, while to the left a further door leads to the dining-room and drawing-room, which are linked by arches either side of the chimney-breast. Although the apartment was superb in its former incarnation, this reworking of the spaces, along with their pared-down simplicity, reflects more accurately the owner's belief in the home being a complete sanctuary, a place where everything is orderly, calm and comfortable. Her love of symmetry is apparent everywhere. Square, boxy shapes predominate but nothing is heavy or too solid. This lightness of touch is achieved by never crowding a room with furniture, but rather choosing appropriate upholstered pieces in neutral tones that contrast with dark-wood tables and stools and the casual arrangements of black-and-white photographs.

4 Lakeside luxury

It sometimes takes a bit of lateral thinking to achieve a perfect result. By buying two adjoining properties the owners of this lakeside apartment in Geneva have created a penthouse of enviable size and character. A Düsseldorf-based designer not only took charge of the building and decoration, but also advised on furniture and pictures; in so doing he has produced a classic and cohesive interior that is full of character and interest. The narrow-planked teak floors are reminiscent of yacht decking and so lend a slightly nautical feel. Instead of a rug for the reception room, a fine taupe carpet made in Belgium was cut and set flush with the boards, tailored and precise. Bookcases slide out on hydraulics for easy access and a wall of two-way mirror conceals a study, at the same time allowing the owner to see through the living-room to the lake beyond. There is a good mixture of antique and contemporary furniture as well as colour and pattern. Wool fabric from Osborne & Little and ethnic prints from Andrew Martin were used for upholstery, while the bedroom walls are lined in cream Pierre Frey flannel. Exquisitely made marble bathrooms and a Bofi kitchen add to the sense of luxury.

classic contemporary

classic contemporary

5 Home and office

Formerly divided into ten dilapidated bed-sits, this four-storey London town house has been designed to accommodate a couple, one of whom is a serious cook, and their three children, as well as an interior design business and a video production company. Everything in the house is made to measure, on a scale that is in keeping with the period building. There are no out-of-bounds areas and the businesses of both partners are housed in the specially kitted-out basement. Old carpets were taken up and the original floorboards sanded and polished or painted. The provision of storage was a high priority throughout the house, as was maximizing any natural light. While open-plan living is popular, there are times when rooms need to be separated, and here, in the ground-floor living area, a pair of large sliding doors can close off the kitchen from the reception room. The workman-like kitchen is a mixture of open shelves, stainless steel and rich mahogany. Sliding doors also separate the main bedroom and bathroom, which has a wall of mirror above the bath, increasing the sense of space two-fold.

classic contemporary

classic contemporary

6 Home and away

Living in Hong Kong but planning in the long term to return to England as their children reached school age, a couple enlisted the help of the wife's father, a recently retired architect, to find a perfect family home. The brief stipulated that it had to have easy access to London, a great view and plenty of space and light – a tall order, but one that produced an admirable result. Prepared to undertake extensive work, they found a country house in a perfect location down a quiet lane in Surrey. The architect and his daughter, a designer, set about the plans, largely by fax and telephone. The rather uninspiring farmhouse was turned into an enviably large light home with an elegant façade, which included the construction of a double-height Regency-style curved front. Old barns were demolished to create a vast kitchen and informal dining area, beyond which are a family sitting-room, the designer's office and garages. There is a lightness of touch about the interiors that reminds one of colonial living – few curtains, cotton slip-covered furniture, Asian antiques and coir matting on bare floorboards. The bedrooms are pale but cosy, with marble bathrooms.

classic contemporary

7 Award winning

Voted the *Sunday Times* Building of the Year in 1995, this exciting and innovative house is set on a coastal rocky site in south-west England. It is rare to find such a unique coastal plot on which to build a new house, but in this case a rambling Victorian house was demolished to make way for an inspired contemporary design. A London-based architectural practice was commissioned by the owner to produce plans for a house that would work as a frequently visited, year-round holiday home. Naturally, the focus is on the exceptional sea views, and the varying levels of the site are used to maximize these and provide a superb flow of movement between the living areas and bedrooms. The raised living-room overlooks the dining area. During good weather an enormous wall of glass can be lowered hydraulically into the ground to open the house dramatically to the steep garden beyond. The floors are of tile, stone or oak, all in natural colours, and marine blue features as a powerful accent colour. There is a wonderful mix of materials, including an ancient-looking structural granite column, which supports the floor and fireplace above.

classic contemporary

classic contemporary

8 Berkeley Square

If plenty of light and a good location are today's most desirable elements when looking for a property, particularly in a city, then this penthouse in London's Berkeley Square has it all. Set on the seventh and eighth floors of an elegant period building, it was stripped back to the brickwork and painstakingly rebuilt using the finest materials and latest technology. From the black-and-white marble entrance-hall, double doors lead to the drawing-room on the left and the kitchen and dining-room on the right. A set of electrically operated glass doors close off the kitchen when required. Full-height glazed doors open on to a hardwood-decked terrace, where the square's two-hundred-year-old plane trees almost touch the railings. The decoration focuses not on pattern or colour but on the various textures of walnut flooring, stainless steel in the kitchen, fine marbles for the bathrooms, mirrors, and the tactile surfaces of suede, cashmere, leather and linen for upholstery. Much of the furniture and lighting was custom-made for the three-bedroom apartment, the owner preferring simple shapes and strong lines, and favouring highly grained hardwoods, ebonized finishes and glass table-tops. There is a sense of the luxury hotel here, and in fact certain hotels provided the impetus for the design brief.

classic contemporary

classic contemporary

9 Home from home

Moving from the United States to the notoriously cramped city of London can be a spatially challenging exercise, and the interior designer who lives in this Chelsea apartment was well aware that finding a large apartment, all on one floor, would take some time. Situated on Sloane Square and designed by the architect Lord Willet in 1900, the building, including an original cage-type lift, has the air of a nineteenth-century gentleman's club. Tall mahogany doors, polished oak floors and finely detailed mouldings and fire-surrounds lend a powerful period atmosphere, but the bathrooms and kitchen are utterly of the twenty-first century. Impressed by the way English designers mix antique and contemporary pieces so successfully, the designer set about adding to her classic American collection. A French marble-topped table, British Arts and Crafts lamps, a Regency mirror and an eighteenth-century Swedish commode all look completely at home in their crisp white surroundings. The owner has also commissioned several items of her own design based on her extensive travels, research into period decoration and time spent in many of the great European art galleries.

classic contemporary

10 Classical order

It is said that a good building becomes outstanding when it achieves a marriage of the functional and the artistic within a human scale. Many people believe that Classicism is the apogee of architectural endeavour; indeed, the Classical Revival, the emulation of Greek and Roman art and architecture, has been almost continuous since the eighth and ninth centuries. A well-known British architect and exponent of the Classical orders designed and built this country house on the established principles of noble simplicity. Although small in scale, it appears larger than it really is, partly because of perfect proportions but also because the architect designed a good deal of the furniture, thus providing a rare continuity of scale and style. This was common practice in the eighteenth and nineteenth centuries when an architect's commission would include all the key pieces of furniture in the public rooms of a house. It is a light home, owing to the large oval or rectangular windows and doors that lead to the terraces, and the inclusion of a glass dome set above the staircase. There is a slightly Empire feel to the interior and yet the house functions as a thoroughly contemporary structure.

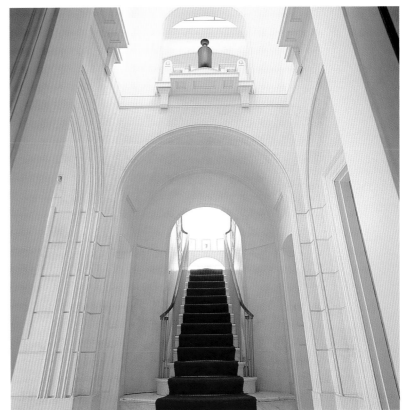

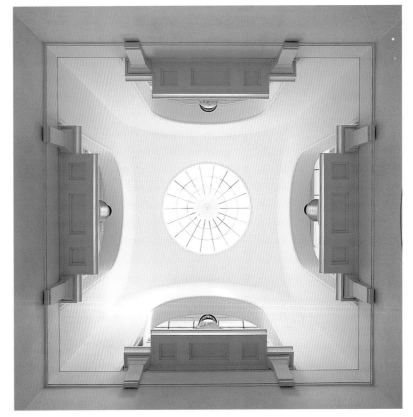

classic contemporary

11 Reflection therapy

Lustre and light are the dominant features of this Thames-side apartment within a new landmark London building. The regeneration of the southern side of the Thames has produced some of the most exciting residential architecture in the UK, and continues to do so. Completed in 2003 on the site of an old flour mill, the 103 apartments, in five connected blocks, are set on a north–south diagonal alignment, all with west-facing views. The designer has capitalized on the amount of glass in the building and the reflective quality of the river to produce a contemporary interior of subtlety and sheen. Metallic wall-finishes glow, satin and silk were used for upholstery, and the colours are that of the ever-changing sky, in soft grey, blue and lavender turning to pink, with natural wood tones adding weight to the pale colour-scheme. Folding doors enable the spaces to be opened up for entertaining, and there is copious storage space. Careful attention has been paid to the whole, where square chairs and sofas echo grid-like book shelves and side-tables, and the mixture of diagonal and vertical lines appears to expand each space. Achieving such balance required much of the interior to be custom-made.

classic contemporary

classic contemporary

12 Peak practice

Everything about this highly individual and unusual home and business is a surprise. It is in the Peak District National Park, near the English city of Sheffield, and has been created from a group of old industrial buildings that have been converted to include a manufacturing enterprise, a shop, a home and a studio. The live/work ethic has always appealed to some people, and here a former gas plant and ancillary buildings have been turned into a glorious property through the vision of its owners and their architect. Two rectangular stone buildings are linked at first-floor level. One, the owner's home, contains bedrooms and bathrooms at ground level and an open-plan kitchen, dining and living area lit from above by glass sections set into the timber-lined roof. The adjacent building houses a studio on the first floor, which is furnished with Eames and Alvar Aalto chairs and an Arts and Crafts sideboard, as well as an extensive collection of books, which are wonderfully accessible, stored in library-style open shelving units. Below the cavernous studio is the shop, and beside this group of buildings is an award-winning round stone structure where the design and manufacture of cutlery takes place. To live and work within a national park is a rare treat.

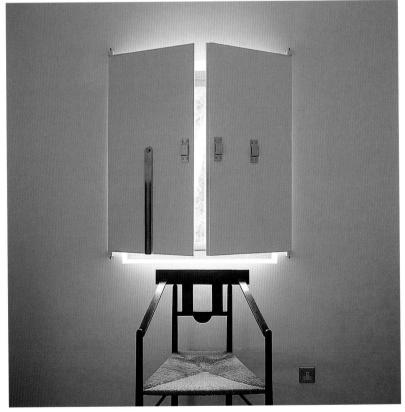

classic contemporary

13 London light

When it was bought, this spacious penthouse overlooking the River Thames in west London was an empty shell; with not even a staircase linking what would become two levels. An architect and his client were therefore able to divide the space without constraint. The interior designer started from scratch and took her inspiration from the often grey and white watery scene beyond. A wall of enormous windows lights the main living spaces, but also, for night-time drama, a lighting designer was called in to provide a complex mix of effects. A broad range of materials in a neutral palette was used to create changes of tempo and colour throughout the interior. Pale oak sliding panels divide the hall from the kitchen, and floors are either oak or limestone, with carpeting in the bedrooms and media area. A walnut panel provides a backdrop to the glass-topped desk in the study, while the media-room walls are lined with crocodile leather. Although quite masculine in style, there is a softness apparent in the choice of cashmere, mohair and satin for bedroom curtains, of grass paper for the walls, and of a curvy 1940s-inspired chair to balance the large boxy sofas.

classic contemporary

classic contemporary

14 Arts and Crafts restoration

The late nineteenth-century Arts and Crafts movement celebrated the revival of handicrafts and the reform of architecture by using traditional crafts and local materials. Inspired by John Ruskin and William Morris and followed by Philip Webb, Norman Shaw and others, the movement declined in England after 1900 but remained influential in Europe and the United States. This listed London house was designed by C.R. Ashbee to accommodate three light-filled working studios. The owner was determined to remove later accretions and was fortunate to discover the original plans, which had been lodged with the Royal Institute of British Architects. Planning restrictions meant that the only alterations allowed were the insertion of new windows in the kitchen and doors to the garden. The major attraction of this house, apart from the superb light, was the amount of wall space on which to display the owner's collection of contemporary art. Furnishings comprise neutral design classics teamed with eighteenth-century French and sixteenth-century Italian antiques. The large living-room includes a sofa and woodblock tables by Christian Liaigre, chairs by Romeo Sozzi and white stools by Tom Critton.

classic contemporary

classic contemporary

15 On Nantucket

A London-based German interior designer and her family spend their holidays on the island of Nantucket, in a house that was just a tiny two-bedroom cottage. She discovered that it could be enlarged and took on the project herself, with the help of an architect who, critically, could advise on any planning restrictions. There are many historic buildings on the island and preserving the vernacular style was important. The roof space was opened up and a large garage converted to become a kitchen (with an Aga set into a niche) and a spacious dining-room. The attic provided several bedrooms and bathrooms. As the house is used year-round the owner included a fireplace, which has full-height bookshelves on either side. The interior decoration suits the location, only minutes from the beach: pine floorboards, white Lloyd Loom furniture and striped cotton-covered sofas are relaxed and casual, and the tongue-and-groove boarding suits the mood and the architecture. Mixing contemporary furniture with several antique pieces gives a holiday home a feeling of permanence and provides a change of shape and texture in such a neutral background.

classic contemporary

16   Neo-classical

One can fantasize about the perfect home, endlessly designing in one's mind and pretending that compromise does not matter, but for one couple it was a single photograph in an estate agent's window that made a dream come true. South London contains a wealth of early twentieth-century houses, built at a time when proportion and detail mattered and quality finishing was the norm. The photograph, however, showed only an elegant bath set before a pair of French doors and a tantalizing view of greenery beyond. Fortunately, apart from some surprising colour-schemes, the rest of the house was as perfect as the bathroom: structurally sound, light and with Neo-classical detailing, it would only need painting from top to bottom. Using a range of grey-toned off-whites, the four-storey house was instantly changed from being rather intimidating and dramatic to a contemporary and comfortable home. Some of the furniture was specially made for the house, but the owners also have a shop supplying their favourite styles from Italy and France, so the ensemble is interesting and original. It is a rare treat to find a large house that works so well without having to carry out major work.

classic contemporary

classic contemporary

17 Personal space

Virtually everything within this Hamburg apartment was designed by the owner, a furniture, textile and interior designer who works in both the domestic market and for commercial and retail clients. Her well-proportioned rooms in a building on the Alster are all painted white, but there are plenty of contrasting colours, numerous textures and original ideas. She is influenced by India and Asia and uses mostly sustainable tropical hardwoods for her furniture. She likes to punctuate bright, white spaces with dark, low tables, floor-cushions in mohair or linen from Dominique Kieffer, and natural or embroidered leather. Great care is taken to set various scenes that invite relaxation and calm. Numerous tea-lights, set in hand-painted glasses by an artist called Gosha, are grouped to set the mood for intimate conversations. There is little pattern, just a bold stripe for the kitchen blind and a quiet print for the generous living-room curtains. This is decoration aimed specifically to relax the owners and bring balance to their busy lives, and is a style that has been eagerly adopted by many people who require a bolt-hole from the outside world.

classic contemporary

18 American classic

Columbia County, north of New York City, contains a wealth of historic architecture, including numerous nineteenth-century houses that have retained their integrity despite often being on the verge of collapse. An artist and restorer, who makes no distinction between fine and applied arts, undertook this renovation in the spirit of the 1820s Federal style, rather than trying to re-create absolute period detailing. The layout is typical of the date, with a good central hall and a four-over-four configuration. All the essential services had to be renewed; walls, floors and ceilings were stripped and redecorated; and the bathrooms and kitchen were all replaced. Although the palette is neutral, the owner has applied various painting techniques to give the impression of aged painted surfaces: broken whites, bleached floorboards and scraped-back pressed-tin ceilings that are left with a mottled finish. Furniture and objets d'art span the Neo-classical, Regency and Biedermeier periods, chosen for their strong presence and simple, functional design. There are collections of old photographs, African masks and plaster busts, and plenty of books. Little colour has been used; the interior relies instead on natural textures and changing light levels.

classic contemporary

19 Town and country

Not every London architect would feel happy to find him or herself in a Victorian country house, but this former city resident relishes the space and the garden. His work takes him back to London frequently but his wife, a horsewoman, and their two children are delighted to live in such a fine period house. He was especially pleased that little had been done to the place, allowing a complete and cohesive refurbishment. Although the interiors are pure white and the finishes contemporary, the house has a gentle edge to it and perhaps more texture than is usual when architects design for themselves. Because there is plenty of space, the compromises of town architecture do not apply in the country. Rooms can have defined purposes: bathrooms are usually converted from bedrooms, kitchens have separate pantries or sculleries, and utility areas do not have to be squeezed into kitchens. All the windows feature walnut-coloured slatted blinds and all the ground-floor rooms are finished in limestone. The good-quality classic materials give the house a timelessness: colour can come and go, furniture may be old or new, fashions may change but this is a house with excellent 'bones'.

classic contemporary

20 Natural conclusion

The wooded rocky landscape of south-east Mallorca was the natural choice for a sculptor wanting to build a new house on the island. She was determined not to destroy the site in any way, and planned the design and construction in order to maximize the use of contemporary green technologies. The conservation of water was a particularly important aspect of the design. Part of the building already existed (a house built about seventy years ago), to which was added an adjoining structure built of the local stone, steel and glass. All the floors are polished stone, some of the internal walls were left in their rough stone state, while others were rendered with a mix of finely ground stone and cement. No paint was used, the pale colour throughout gained from the natural materials. Apart from an old English lounger, most of the furniture was bought on the island: simple white cotton-covered sofas and cane chairs and a pure-white marble dining table. The timber ceiling beams are original to the old house, and all the doors and windows have wooden frames, but the new wing, housing the bedrooms and bathrooms, features frameless openings. The owner, who works in steel, lead, wood and stone, has created an admirable year-round dwelling completely at one with the land.

classic contemporary

21 Spot on

The exuberant and colourful interior of this house belies its difficult site and limited size. Mews houses were never designed for family life but the architect and interior designer employed to transform this London property came up with some clever ideas. The key to the project was the design of an inner courtyard that would allow light and, crucially, fresh air into the house. The front façade is protected but everything behind it was completely rebuilt, the courtyard, or atrium, becoming a focal point as part garden and part work of art. The use of large sections of glass brings in the light, and walls of mirrored glass inside reflect and enlarge the spaces. Sliding glass doors and an electronically operated glass roof allow the house to be opened up or closed according to the weather. This kind of flexibility has only recently been made possible, now that advanced technology enables glass to be used even in a fire zone. A vivid palette of primary colours against a white background looks modern, young and efficient, while spots and circles are an amusing and simple geometric motif.

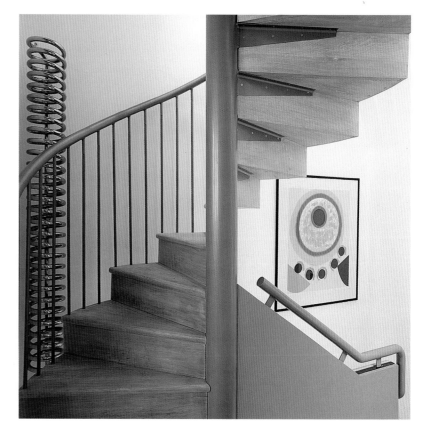

classic contemporary

classic contemporary

22 Light fantastic

Six pairs of impressive French doors give on to a full-width balcony in this first-floor lateral conversion on a famous London garden square. Bought by an American couple after five frustrating years of house-hunting, it required major work and spatial replanning. Apart from the French doors, nothing else survived, and the architect and designer were free to create a highly individual space, the focal point of which is the large drawing-room and connecting library. Instead of a conventional entrance-hall the front door opens into a good-sized lobby with double doors to both dining-room ahead and drawing-room to the left. A double-volume space was created in the master bathroom by lowering the ceiling and building storage above. A dressing-room fills the space beyond the bathroom, set either side of a pair of French doors. Every detail was studied in great depth: skirting-boards have been sized correctly, doors made to the right proportions and mirrored glass used to great effect. This is a family home designed to suit the owners' lifestyle perfectly.

classic contemporary

23 Timeless teamwork

As houses and apartments go through countless refurbishments and changing fashions, details such as picture- and dado-rails come and go, radiators are boxed over or left exposed and, of course, kitchens and bathrooms are replaced at an astonishing rate. Working in the international fashion business means that the owners of this central London apartment travel frequently. They did not want any of the fussy Victorian detail they found, except the plasterwork ceilings in the principal rooms, and they asked a design partnership to create a completely new look for the apartment based on neutral colours, contemporary design and various items bought in anticipation of the refurbishment. Neither minimalist nor crowded, the interiors are a beautifully balanced composition of light and space, texture and tone, and above all, it is a look that is difficult to date. Contemporary furniture mixes comfortably with antiques, and the whole apartment is treated as a single space, rather like a uniquely luxurious and spacious hotel suite. What more could one dream of in central London?

classic contemporary

24   Perfect pied-à-terre

To live in a country house and acquire a bolt-hole in the city is the dream of many. The city apartment can be quite different from the country property, is probably much smaller, and perhaps decorated more whimsically or with colours not tried before. Bought as a wreck by a young interior designer for her own use several days a week, this smart one-bedroom flat overlooking the Chelsea Physic Garden in central London fits the bill in all ways. It has a view, plenty of light, good storage and feels much bigger than it really is. The entire space had to be gutted, the rooms turned back to front, and the floors raised to allow new plumbing to a luxurious new bathroom. Good design has been employed to maximize the scale of each room. It is no good having high ceilings and large windows if the rooms are divided into spaces that are too small, and the temptation to squeeze in a second bedroom should be abandoned in favour of fewer and better areas for living.

classic contemporary

25 Tone and texture

The owner of this spacious apartment in one of London's premier squares turned to an old friend to advise on every aspect of the interior design. The designer divides her time between working in finance and dealing in antique Asian and Ottoman textiles, and well understood that the apartment on the lower-ground and ground floors should provide a calm environment as well as a place to hang a growing collection of works of art. A beautifully balanced mix of contemporary and antique furniture was chosen by the pair in Paris, Hong Kong and London. Certain items such as side-tables, headboards and cupboards were custom-made and covered in various leathers and vellum, tactile and rich. Twentieth-century pieces are prominent: plates by Duncan Grant, 1920s mirrors, and tables from the 1950s work well against the contemporary and neutral backdrop of pale painted walls and wooden floors. High-quality finishing and attention to the smallest detail is evident throughout. Much is made of texture in design today and the contrasts here between leather, silk, velvet, shagreen, polished hardwoods, bronze and hand-woven Turkish fabrics are an important element in the overall design.

classic contemporary

classic contemporary

26 Radical regeneration

A forlorn semi-detached cottage in Twickenham, south-west London, is the latest home of a young German architect. He had realized the potential of the house while previously living opposite. Although it had been untouched since the 1940s, with no bathroom and only an outside WC, he could see that the warren of small rooms could be reconfigured and a radical transformation would be possible. Every inch of space was studied in great detail and many innovative ideas introduced. The hall was widened; an outer wall was pushed into a narrow side passage and the newly formed dining area was lit from above by glass panels inserted into the roof. Instead of a conventional set of doors, a wall of glass now opens the ground floor to the garden. The staircase wall was also removed, allowing light onto the stairs and room for plenty of built-in seating beneath. A partly open-plan kitchen runs along one wall with a laundry concealed by cupboards at one end. From what appeared to be some impossibly small spaces on the upper level, there is now a master bedroom, luxurious bathroom, a further bedroom and a large sleeping-platform inserted under the roof and reached by a ladder. This transformation beautifully illustrates how cramped old houses can easily adapt to contemporary living, given the right architectural vision and building skills.

classic contemporary

27 Safe as houses

Hidden behind the elegant but conventional façade of a four-storey Victorian town house in Belgravia, London, is one of the most technologically advanced homes around. Designed as a state-of-the-art environment, with everything from climate control to bullet-proof CCTV cameras (giving digital images that can be accessed from anywhere in the world), this house virtually thinks for its owner. This is interior design that has moved far beyond the usual makeover. The integral garage features a turntable for easy manoeuvring; a home cinema and steam-room are now essential; and luxury bathing in this case means a circular teak bathtub of gigantic size. Not only is the technology right up-to-date, but every inch of space is maximized and designed to function with speed and convenience. The office is set up as a 'smart home', and global, top-name brands were used for the kitchen, sound systems, lighting and entertainment. Bespoke design and fine craftsmanship are important aspects of interior design today, and here the most outstanding fixture is a crystal chandelier, made up of over 1000 individual pieces, which hangs through three floors of the stairwell. Leather floors, fine marble bathrooms, high-pressure showers, enormous champagne fridges and luxury fabrics are no longer unusual elements of contemporary design in houses such as this.

classic contemporary

classic contemporary

eclectic 28–44

Decorating doyenne

Moving from a house to an apartment can be a difficult experience but this is a very special lateral conversion that suits its owner's needs to perfection. Belonging to a greatly respected and internationally recognized London decorator, who bought two apartments to create the layout she wanted, it would rightly be many people's idea of the perfect city home. Famously generous and fond of entertaining, she has arranged her apartment roughly as two hotel-like suites, with the main focus on generous reception and dining areas, linked by openings either side of a fireplace. She is a master of colour and scale, and one of the best in the business at combining old and new styles. Many of the fabrics and paint colours are from her own ranges, and favourite pieces of furniture move with her from house to house, providing a comforting continuity. She has used mirrored glass on a grand scale, which enhances the already light-filled rooms. The dining-hall wall is almost filled by a William Yeoward oak china-cabinet, and above the sofa in the sitting-room hangs a giant antique panelled mirror. The predominant gentle colours of pale blue, rich green, cream and amethyst are original, modern and chic.

eclectic

Singular success

29

Instead of trying to make his vertical space look larger by using the common device of an all-white scheme, the interior design director of a top UK fabric and design company took another approach in this south-west London apartment. A developer had bought an old school, divided the spaces into units of various sizes and sold them on as empty shells. From the entrance-hall, the staircase, with one wall covered in a floral paper, leads to a mezzanine level. On the left is a wall of bookcases, and further on an ingenious bathroom created by using screens so that one can see partially beyond the square washbasin and bath into the bedroom. Solid walls would have meant small box-like rooms and too many doors. The library is visible from the ground floor through a wire balustrade stretched across the open space. Solid blocks of colour define the spaces, anchored by a dark wall in the dining area, which is furnished with an octagonal antique table and chrome chairs. The kitchen is a smooth strip of timber and slate, which runs unobtrusively along one wall in the living-room. This is a beautifully designed space, full of panache.

eclectic

30 Regency revival

This London house is situated in a fine Regency terrace. The exterior was in excellent shape but the designer, who was called on to create an elegant home from scratch, described the interior as a mess. There is little evidence now of just how much work was required to reinstate the interiors, including remaking the staircase, restoring architraves and cornices, altering the doors, designing a new kitchen, and much else besides. The owners were scaling down from a much larger and grander house, and together with their designer they chose favourite pictures and furniture from their large collection of fine pieces. Immediately striking is the high-quality workmanship throughout, from the floors to the specially made shutters in the drawing-room: painted a French blue, they were designed to open top and bottom, thereby allowing control over the amount of light in the room. Bathrooms are old-fashioned but extremely comfortable. There is a mix of contemporary carpets by Sandy Jones and an Oriental rug in the dining-room. Artworks include an Oriel Harwood head and pictures by Paul Nash and James Pryde. This is a sophisticated but relaxed home indeed.

31 Fabric house

The owner of this house near Hof in Germany was fortunate enough to be able to build virtually anything he wanted. His business, the manufacture of luxurious textiles for an international clientèle, is housed in immaculate premises in the rural and agricultural district where he now lives. His quirky collections of chairs and sofas are nearly all covered in his own velvets, grouped not according to some carefully studied colour-scheme but for their contrasting colour and shape. The house, set among rolling lawns and gardens, looks as if it has always been there, though the interiors are contemporary and extremely well designed for twenty-first-century living. Of many great details to be found here, the wine cellar, reached via a circular stone staircase, is the most spectacular, but all the rooms contain unusual pictures, prints, sculptures, mirrors and collections of books. The owner has a rare ability to mix items of vastly differing provenance in a relaxed but exciting way. There are changes in mood from summer to winter, bold colour to pure-white walls and simple wooden floors. Above all, the spaces are luxurious and stimulating.

eclectic

Design icons

Space tends to dictate how rooms are furnished, and the owner of this large west London house, a furniture designer whose work is artistic and sculptural, has used his luxurious light-filled rooms to display a collection of his own work and some of his favourite twentieth-century design icons. The high ceilings, tall windows and pale floors are almost gallery-like, the white-painted walls a perfect foil for the sometimes eccentric and powerful shapes of each piece. He has successfully combined graphic cube-like elements with sensuous rounded pieces, all designed within the last century. The exception is an antique writing-table set near a window in the living-room. There are chairs from Bugatti, André Dubreuil and Frank Gehry, each piece an individual work of art, but incorporated into a pleasing ensemble of texture, shape and colour. Understanding scale is important, and where original details such as the skirting-boards are present, the owner has been careful to include radiator covers of appropriate proportions. Existing fire surrounds are simple and classic. Once again, this house highlights the successful marriage of period architecture and a highly individual choice of furniture and art.

eclectic

eclectic

33 Euro style

Located in an enviable position on London's Chelsea Embankment, this substantial corner house has sweeping river views, large rooms and appropriately high ceilings. A complete redesign and refurbishment was carried out by a Munich-based designer for her German client, whose brief focused on total comfort and relaxation. She has achieved a synthesis between a very classic European style combined with Asian antiques and the owner's memorabilia. The most striking aspect of the house are the enormous windows in the double-aspect living-room, which are luxuriously curtained in a cream-and-caramel striped fabric from Andrew Martin. This fabric was the anchor on which the colour-scheme was established. The floors are covered in fine Persian rugs and the furniture is upholstered in a silk-and-wool fabric. Many of the choice antiques were bought by the designer, including the tall gilt Baroque mirror frame that leans on the study wall framing an artwork created by the designer. She also sourced the many Chinese pieces and the pair of Indian stone columns in the hall. A stay at the Hempel Hotel in London inspired the decoration of the ivory-and-red master bedroom, a vibrant departure from the warm whites throughout the rest of the house.

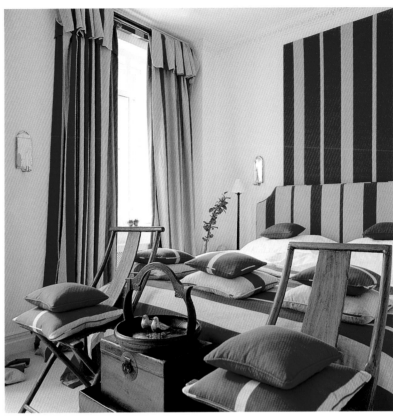

34 Cool classic

There are entire streets in London where so little has changed that one marvels at the sense of having stepped back in time. Newly painted, unusually coloured front doors are sometimes the only clue that the nineteenth century has well and truly gone, and that owners today live in a quite different way from their Victorian or Georgian predecessors. Completely undaunted by the elaborate Victorian interior of this house, the new owners bought it on the strength of its wonderful windows and a layout of rooms that worked particularly well for their needs. Much original detailing survived, and the designer—owner was convinced that her neutral, contemporary style would complement the good marble fireplaces, mouldings, staircase and shutters. Furnished with a mix of French and Italian antiques, plus modern sofas and chairs, the house is imbued with an understated luxury. African artefacts, contemporary minimalist works of art and a limited colour palette create a calm but interesting backdrop to family life. Oak and stone floors are softened by a collection of bold rugs from Oriental Heritage in London, anchoring the neutral linens and woods on a rich stripy ground.

eclectic

35 Queen Anne

There is an enclave of wonderfully preserved red-brick houses near the River Thames in Chiswick, west London. Narrow streets lead to the river in an area that was much favoured by eighteenth-century merchants and traders, many of whose homes have survived in a surprisingly cohesive group. The twentieth century, though, was a time when respect for period architecture dropped to a low ebb, social conditions changed rapidly and few large houses remained intact. The owners of this now beautifully restored period piece realized that it would make an ideal family home, even though it was in poor condition. Restoring the original proportions of each room was a priority, as was the replacement or repair of existing features such as the wall-panelling, the shutters and the timber floors, which were stripped. The kitchen was moved from what is now the dining-room to the back of the house. A pair of tall French doors gives on to an old stone terrace and the long, narrow garden, which has a simplicity and elegance to echo that of the house. The mix of pale sandy paint colours, patterned wallpapers and pretty antique furniture proves that an eclectic approach to design and a sensitivity to architectural features make old houses into dream homes for many.

eclectic

36 The collector

Being a collector can sometimes feel like a burden. To begin with, it can be difficult to find homes for an ever-growing number of items, whether chairs, bowls, fossils or rugs. One man's solution has been virtually to give over his entire early nineteenth-century house to a sometimes eccentric but always inspiring collection of objects. Every room is crammed with auction-house finds or items that simply have a special colour or texture. He derives enormous pleasure from his four-storey house with its bare floorboards and uncurtained windows. Every room is painted white, apart from the ground-floor dining-room, where he has lined the walls with sweet-smelling timber, reminiscent of a cigar box. The final finish may be left as it is or chosen from an ambiguous little sample of something found on the beach or at a local shop. Having plenty of space to arrange tablescapes, turn columns on their side or just fill corners with mirrors or chairs is deemed by the collector to be pure luxury. Shape and patina are everything, whether the latest delight be a garden stool or a fine Regency table.

37 Mews magic

Mews were generally built to house stables, and later on garages, at
street level, with fodder storage and basic accommodation for
coachmen or drivers above. In the twentieth century they rapidly
became highly sought-after city dwellings, set quietly, for the most part,
behind the grander houses to which they belonged, across a cobbled
street or lane. Planning regulations generally insist on the old garage
doors remaining intact to preserve the historic sense of a mews, but in
some cases the ground-floor premises are now shops. Because the
accommodation was originally a simple set of rooms without much in
the way of architectural features, owners have been able to create
virtually any sort of interior they desire. The owner of this London house
has a shop specializing in Gustavian furniture and objets d'art, and has
decorated it in her favourite style, mixing in French and English pieces.
Light and bright, it is filled with glorious eighteenth-century distressed
cupboards, tables, chairs and clocks. The paleness is enlivened by
touches of gilt, coloured tiles, textiles and fresh flowers.

eclectic

38 Fulham pride

Although this house, set in a Victorian terrace in Fulham, west London, is not large, the proportions of every room are ideal. A well-respected designer was asked to improve the layout, design new bathrooms and suggest furniture and fabrics for the young owner. Some period detailing survived and has been retained in the principal rooms, adding an elegance that does not come with newly built properties. High ceilings and wonderful windows are major features so curtains and poles were kept simple, relying on stripes to provide a graphic look. Strong blocks of colour and plenty of black detailing in the sitting-room and dining area are classic decorative motifs, here refined by the choice of a glass-topped table and chairs that have an outdoor-café look. An entire floor was allocated for the master suite of bedroom and bathroom, and, taking advantage of the ceiling height, Venetian-style poles were used to create a dramatic and original four-poster bed. The bathroom incorporates plenty of storage and is enviably light. As well as a guest suite, the top of the house has been given over to a sleek studio space, purpose built for the artist–owner and lit by plenty of ceiling lights.

39 Light control

An Ibizan shop owner and designer has built a reputation for transforming uninviting and run-down houses into desirable and architecturally innovative homes. A recent project has turned a very ordinary building into a spacious Modernist-style property using cool materials, expanses of glass and interesting changes of volume. Palm trees surround the two-storey coastal property, which has marvellous views over a bay and ancient castle. White-painted walls predominate, but natural-coloured polished-plaster finishes cover some walls and the chunky, smooth platforms used as bedheads and space dividers. Fond of a broad range of Asian artefacts, the owner has placed stools, chairs, plant-holders and even small boats throughout the house, relying on their naturalistic shapes and colours for both functional and decorative effect. The mixture of window shapes, from tall and narrow to shallow and wide, creates an interesting play of light throughout the house. Bedrooms are removed from the public areas, and the kitchen is set behind a row of pillars off the main living-room, in a cool recess. Above all, the designer's use and control of natural light is the outstanding feature of this most covetable home.

eclectic

40   Artistic triumph

Mindful that a collection of modern art should not create a museum-like atmosphere, a London-based interior designer has thoughtfully combined furniture, lamps, rugs and sculpture in a loose and very twentieth-century manner. Inspired by Kettle's Yard, Jim Ede's private museum of twentieth-century art in Cambridge, this first-floor apartment is set out in a free-form manner, unusual in this early nineteenth-century space. For the drawing-room, the largest space in the apartment, Sandy Jones designed cushions and carpets in the Modernist style. A new fireplace was installed, designed to be a bridge between the contents of the room and its architecture, and works by Sean Scully and Robert Motherwell hang on the same wall. There are Arne Jacobsen chairs and behind them a striking painting by Howard Hodgkin. The study is imbued with a powerful African influence, the reductionist forms of which had a major effect on our twentieth-century visual vocabulary. A pair of 1930s French python-skin chairs is set beside a palm-wood and ebony desk; beneath them lies a chequered Sandy Jones rug. The bedroom contains a collection of paintings from the 1960s, including Kenneth Noland's *Target* and a vertical stripe by Morris Louis, which hang above and beside a country Chippendale chest.

eclectic

41 Calm confidence

A busy couple who work in London during the week but retreat to an Oxfordshire country house at weekends have created a town house that is a perfect antidote to their high-speed city lives. The house was bought, in part, for its garden, so that three terriers could happily commute with their owners. The property, not far from the Houses of Parliament, had not had much attention since the 1960s so a major refurbishment and extension was carried out. All the designing was undertaken by the owners but when it came to colour and fabrics they enlisted the help of an interior decorator. Reclaimed nineteenth-century flagstones were laid in the entrance-hall, which was extended to create a conservatory-style dining-room. The decoration has an Oriental touch, seen in the use of rattan from OKA, Asian antiques and black lacquer. The main bedroom features 1930s chinoiserie fabric. Although many items were bought for the house, the walls are filled with interesting family collections of pictures, including a number of Stanley Spencer drawings. Colours are soft and pattern is limited to several Persian rugs and striped velvets and silks. Shape is an important factor in elements such as the curvy chairs, Oriental jars and pots, and in the way objects are grouped.

42 Gilt edged

A gallery owner, picture-framing expert and author of several design books has decorated her large London apartment in pale, creamy whites, concentrating on the play of natural light afforded by its luxuriously tall windows. Instead of a separate dining-room she has been able to incorporate an antique table and chairs into the new kitchen, a popular change from the conventional idea that eating in the kitchen is for family only. An open wine rack, surrounded by numerous pictures, gives the room a special ambience and interest. In a departure from the neutral palette, an intense but distressed blue highlights the central island unit. During the research and writing of her book on contemporary curtains the owner discovered new, lighter window treatments that would filter and diffuse light, rather than block out this most precious commodity. Layered sheer fabrics and antique lace hang in the drawing-room, soft veil-like organza and pashmina in the bedroom. The mix of antique furniture and gilt picture-frames and mirrors creates an utterly soothing and feminine interior.

eclectic

43 Town house

Nothing but a weathered old door and a single window can be seen from the street. It would appear that only a tiny and very narrow house could be squeezed into such a tight space, but ancient Provençal towns and villages are full of surprises. The front door opens onto another world: the dimly lit, tiled hall leads to a stone staircase that draws one up to a magnificent enclosed courtyard garden, two sides of which are formed by the house itself. The adjacent town wall is certainly thirteenth-century and the house was known to have been a resting-place for members of the church travelling from Rome to Avignon to visit the Pope. The poet, scientist and doctor Nostradamus was born near by. The present owners, who are Dutch, called in an expert and highly respected architectural practice situated only a few buildings away to carry out a complete renovation and redesign. Masters of the Provençal vernacular, the team has built a most elegant home from somewhat inauspicious beginnings. The mainly French and English furnishings and fabrics were chosen by the owners to complement the typically eighteenth-century-French greys and muted pastels of the flat paintwork – a timeless combination.

eclectic

44 Painter's palette

Paint is the most cost-effective way of decorating, and a young American artist has completely transformed her home in Notting Hill, London, by painting the floors, walls, tiles and most of the furniture. Instead of sticking to a safely neutral palette, she chose a mixture of red, aubergine, charcoal, pebble and several shades of white. The horizontal textured stripes in the sitting-room were inspired by a house in Beirut, and by continuing the stripes across a pair of built-in 1980s cupboards they recede and the room appears larger. The ground-floor study is red and the cloakroom deep aubergine. Elsewhere, the house is pale and light, particularly the kitchen/dining-room. Auction finds and inexpensive pine furniture are all painted white, but a changing collection of works of art by the owner and her friends brings a vivid shot of colour into the rooms. Upstairs, she used a pale grey in the bedroom and ivory for the bathrooms, both of which were lined in blue tiles, effectively painted in two-tone stripes. The decoration is confident, and the owner clearly knows what she likes and is unafraid to mix old and new.

exotic 45–55

45 Orientalist tradition

Some people are inspired by fashion, others by Continental style or travel, or family heirlooms, but the ceramicist who decorated and lives in this south London house has expanded her work to fill her life. She is considered by many to be the major contemporary representative of the English Orientalist tradition. Her inspiration comes from Ottoman pottery and Iznik patterns: the floral shapes and arabesque leafy scrolls, and above all the wonderful coloured glazes with gold decoration. Her pottery is part of the fabric of the house and displays fill wavy shelves and niches in the walls, which she specially designed and made to show off her varied pieces, as well as a collection of antique work from various periods. Almost the entire house is painted in shades of pink, and even the stair carpet was made to her own design and colourway. The lilac velvet seating areas are piled with cushions, which are hand-painted by the owner. Lampshades receive the same treatment. It is a rare treat to find an interior so utterly of its creator.

46 Traditional manner

A designer and painter chose Northern Cyprus as the ideal location for his holiday home. Formerly the old village coffee-house, this is a handsome building, brought back to life and once again in harmony with the island landscape. Rather than tackle the restoration all at once, it is an evolving process, the allotted annual works undertaken by local people and in the traditional manner, but it is no casual holiday project. Everything is carefully planned and drawn up to guide the workmen. The paints are natural locally available pigments, which are light and vibrant and typical of the Mediterranean, and the original concrete floors have been coloured with diluted oil paint and given a wax polish. It is the sort of house that can absorb an exotic mix of items from numerous countries such as Uzbekistan, India and Egypt, fusing colour and texture; things bought purely for pleasure, over many years, look right here. The East is close at hand and the garden and exterior living spaces reflect that influence. The sound of water trickling into pools creates a wonderfully calm atmosphere and there are numerous sunny or shady areas in which to relax.

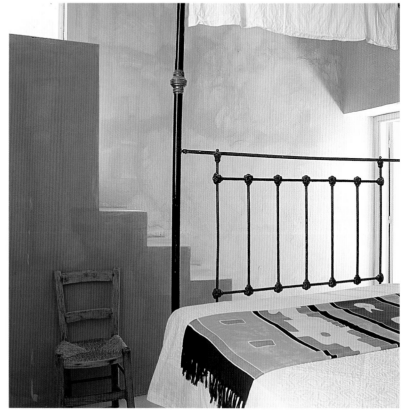

47 Island idyll

The island of St Lucia in the Caribbean is a great place to build a dream home. The many hilly sites afford superb views of the sea, and the climate ensures that any garden becomes a bountiful and colourful tropical splendour. The owner of this house on the coast was inspired to commission its building by his chosen architect's own house in Barbados. The owner's mother, an experienced designer of Caribbean interiors, was on hand to advise on the choice of colour, furniture and decoration, ever mindful of the need for simplicity. Open walkways, guarded by wooden pillars and handrails, curve around the site, allowing cooling sea breezes to penetrate the rooms. The open beamed ceilings look appropriately casual, and almost everything is white: built-in seating and much of the furniture is painted white, and white fabrics have been used for cushions and on the beds. The only colour to be seen, apart from the natural wood tones of the bedsteads and some carved Asian furniture, is a riot of yellow-and-blue tiling in the bathroom, shiny copper pans in the kitchen and blue-and-white table-settings.

48 Cliff-top retreat

One of the best aspects of a holiday home is the fact that the practical issues of everyday life, such as storage space, are largely irrelevant. Utter simplicity is often the key, especially in a warm climate, where the house is almost secondary to the outside. Set on a cliff-top above the sea in Mallorca, this one-room cottage, which only recently gained a supply of running water, was built by the native owner's grandfather. Apart from the plumbing, the grandson has also erected a Moorish-style wall across the width of the cottage to create a sleeping and living area; in one niche is a gas hob, in another a sink, while shelves store basic kitchen equipment. Behind the wall are a tiny shower and WC. The old fireplace, used in the past for cooking and heating, has been retained. Time spent here is mainly on the terraces, which are bedecked with colourful rugs and cushions, and a table with comfortable wicker chairs, to enable the owners to enjoy the views of the sea below.

49 African farm

When it came to building this new house, surrounded by lush lawns and eucalyptus plantations beside a farm dam in Zimbabwe, the owners were inspired by Australian colonial architecture. With no planning restrictions and an ample supply of home-produced bricks and building timbers, the design could be virtually anything they wanted. They decided on a building only one room wide and extremely long, so that every room faces the water, game park and bush beyond, and with the rooms arranged *en enfilade* one can see from one end of its immense length to the other. The central entrance-hall at the rear, decorated in black, yellow and white, connects through doors, either side of a Jacobean cupboard, to the beamed reception room and on to the full-length covered terraces. The house has only one bedroom (garden cottages accommodate guests) and is entirely on one level. The vast roof is made of a modern, pre-finished corrugated iron, which requires no maintenance. The plastered brick masonry is painted in off-white. This new house works perfectly in its high veldt environment, where the near-perfect climate allows year-round indoor and outdoor living.

50 Caribbean style

Many British colonists, builders and architects adapted prevailing Victorian fashions into homes far removed from 'dear old England'. Nostalgia played a large part in colonial architecture around the world, from the Caribbean to Australia and New Zealand. In St Lucia particularly, the 'Gingerbread' house – all lacy fretwork verandas, bargeboards and railings – became the traditional style. This fine example of the genre is in fact a late twentieth-century distillation of a great deal of research and planning by both its former and current owners. Eminently suited to today's lifestyle, the house nonetheless has all the atmosphere and ambience of its historic antecedents. Loft-tray ceilings, hardwood floors and potted palms; blue-and-white china and Oriental cupboards and rugs; fine bone china and sugary paint colours – all combine to create a real sense of history. While most of the furniture in the house was bought in St Lucia and Barbados, some pieces, such as the four-poster beds, were designed by the owner and made locally. The tropical gardens are filled with palms and pink bougainvillaea, and the southerly views are the stuff of dreams.

51 Agrarian dream

The owner of this exotic country house was determined to build it after succumbing to the beauty of the Cape province during a holiday. Two friends, both New York-based architects, came up with a design that echoed an agricultural vernacular, though was far removed from the familiar white-gabled Cape Dutch homesteads of earlier generations. Set above the Paarl valley, the views across numerous vineyards and the farm's olive groves are magnificent. The farmhouse suits the climate perfectly, has expansive entertaining areas, separate guest accommodation and barn-like office and garage space. The dun-coloured render on the walls of the house was inspired by a watercolour painting and was mixed on site. The enormous central living-room is cool and shaded, the waxed grey and ochre concrete floor is divided by strips of dark Balau wood, and the walls are coloured a soft muddy green. Most of the furniture and lighting was bought in Cape Town, although artworks are largely by family and friends. The two-dimensional work above the white sofa is by Lucien Rees-Roberts and the large work in the living-room by Francisco Bustamante Gubbins. Ethnic, antique and contemporary influences combine with local materials, such as the South African slate lining the master bathroom and the khaki twill fabric used for curtains.

52 World traveller

Mallorca is a popular tourist destination and an island where Northern Europeans have bought farmhouses (fincas) for decades. There is an established year-round community, and there are many artists and craftspeople working in the towns and villages. This is not a holiday home but a very old town house in Santanyí, which serves as home and shop for its owner, an antiques dealer who specializes in ethnic carvings, old doors, rugs, sculpture and art, much of which he buys on his travels around the world during the winter. The house works perfectly as home and showroom: the vaulted hallway is used to display smaller items, and there is a very large gallery in the roof space, as well as a garage-like space on the side of the house where cupboards, tables, enormous doors and rugs are on show. Little work had to be carried out, apart from installing a new bathroom and upgrading the lofty kitchen/dining-room, where wall-to-wall banquette seating is covered in rugs and cushions. Cosy and exotic, the decoration is individual and personal. The garden is filled with decorative pots and an abundance of flowering plants. All in all, this is an enchanting place to live and work.

53 Original view

An old quarryman's cottage did not initially seem to have much going for it when a young British ceramicist first found it tucked away in the Forest of Dean in south-west England. It was dark, divided into two, had wobbly additions and had been used as a cider house for years – which explains why the doorways are wider than normal (just a little wider than a cider barrel, to be exact). But those of us driven to expend vast amounts of effort on our homes do not worry about small imperfections.This talented owner first lived in the house, getting to know the light levels and how the rooms would work, leading one to another. Anyone who knows the owner's work will not be surprised to see her idea of a dream interior, using as it does the myriad colours and the rose motif seen on her pots, plates, mugs and bowls. Colour is an abiding passion; white is anathema. There are no pictures on the walls and all the furniture is practical and functional. One must applaud her originality and courage of conviction.

54 Cape classic

To become the owner of an old South African Cape Dutch homestead, set among its own vines, is the dream of many. This rare and extraordinary house has been in the same family for hundreds of years, and its contents reflect that fact. It would be impossible to buy, in a single lifetime, the diverse and eclectic range of objects and furniture that fills every room. It is a house that can be read like a book: page after page of the family's history is displayed, from the earliest arrivals who brought European furniture with them, right up to today as the current owner adds his own choice of pictures, lamps and objets d'art. Those bedrooms and bathrooms that are set under the towering thatched roof are quite different from those on the floors below. Each one somehow takes on the character of its materials and varying light levels. Some rooms appear to be entirely European in origin, others very African, especially where furniture has been locally made of native woods rarely seen in Europe. Bold colour is to be seen everywhere: red leather, pink and blue velvet, yellow and lime-green stripes, and floral patterns are all juxtaposed, and yet nothing bothers the eye. This wonderful house is a compelling cabinet of curiosities.

55 Island character

Leaving Northern Europe behind to live in the sun is probably a recurring dream of millions of people. Those who succeed often find their lives take a completely new course. The refurbishment of this Mallorcan farmhouse so impressed friends and locals that it led its owners to set up an architecture and design business on the island. Two shops also now supply an international clientèle with all manner of antiques, fabrics and furniture, some of which is made to the owners' designs, in both traditional metalwork and wood. The furnishing and decorating of this home set their company's standard for comfortable but casual island living. Mindful of retaining the seventeenth-century character of the house, the modernizing work was carefully controlled, but the landscaping of the large property was a major project. As with most old farmhouses, there were barns attached that could be converted into a summer dining-room or seating area. Dark beams, white walls and painted floors are the background against which colourful dhurries and kelims add warmth and texture. A mix of dark European furniture and neutral contemporary sofas creates a relaxed environment, and plenty of vernacular architectural detailing helps to convey the essential character of this enviable place in the sun.

cool minimalism 56–66

56 White house

Asked by his client to draw up plans to update an old house in Nantucket, an iconic American architect has created a perfectly balanced ensemble to suit the owner's requirements exactly. The exterior was to remain in keeping with the local vernacular by using wooden shingles instead of a painted plaster finish, while the owner stipulated a pure-white interior, contemporary in style, simple, calm and light. The origins of the house have not disappeared altogether as the large coach or garage doors have been retained, but they now have glass doors behind them to let in plenty of light. The remaining windows are not curtained but all have white-painted shutters. Apart from numerous books, there is almost no colour inside or out, although the grey shingles, paving-stones, variations in floor colour and some metal lamps all stand out against the white woodwork, walls and the white upholstered furniture. As dining-rooms are often under-used it was a good idea, practically and decoratively, to fill the walls with bookshelves, which are built in a grid pattern as in a library and repeated along a wall in the main bedroom. Such pure interiors rely on superb design and first-class finishes.

cool minimalism

cool minimalism

57 Spatially aware

Buying off-plan can be a risky business, but this apartment was purchased without a plan at all, just an empty space with walls, plenty of windows and a roof. The owners spend a lot of time in California and were concerned that wherever they lived in London would never be light enough. The solution was a roof-top above a warehouse conversion. It was never intended that it should remain as one vast open space but months were spent working out how light moved across the building and where the required divisions should be sited. Once the rooms were mapped out, the owners set about putting up walls, painting the floors (in white of course) and installing heating and lighting systems. The apartment now includes three bedrooms with bathrooms, a very large living-room and a kitchen with an outer wall made of curved glass panes set into metal frames. Big-name designers feature prominently. The marble-topped dining-table is by Eero Saarinen and the pair of white leather chairs are B&B Italia. Fortunately there was ample space for storage and large cupboards in the bedrooms, essential in such a pared-down living space where the only colour is white.

cool minimalism

58 Form and function

The Sri Lankan owner of this mid-Victorian London house had very definite ideas about his ideal home: his lifestyle – that of constant international travel – was the driving force behind his need for simplicity. The majority of the work undertaken to convert the semi-derelict property required a like-minded architect and a skilled builder to achieve such a polished result. Much of the design relies on the use of fine materials and a creative exploitation of glass. Instead of removing the hall wall, glass panels were inserted into sections of it, providing a glimpse through to the ground-floor living-room. A section of the stripped pine floor was also removed and replaced with glass, and by hanging two large oil paintings by the same artist above and below the gap a sense of airiness and space was achieved. The basement was opened up to house the kitchen and dining area. A conveyor-belt swathe of American walnut was taken from the window at the front, up and over the island unit, along the floor and formed into the dining-table. The work units behind were custom-made in walnut and stainless steel. Bedrooms and bathrooms are equally seamless and smooth.

cool minimalism

59 Simple pleasure

Even in the frequently dazzling light of the South of France many owners and designers now use massive sheets of glass to link houses seamlessly to their gardens and to expose views in a way that was unheard of in the past. Two Belgian designers took on the challenge of rebuilding these two traditional stuccoed houses, set on a hillside above St Tropez, which they have linked by a new double-height central block. From the outside very little appears to have changed, but internally sheets of glass have been employed in the form of screens, replacing either whole walls or sections of walls, and doors are made of tall panels of glass with simple flat frames. Colour and texture variations are achieved by the use of dark and light woods (mainly cedar) for wall panelling, headboards, bathroom cupboards, doors, tables and window frames. Furniture is contemporary or by well-known Art Nouveau designers. A grey-tiled swimming-pool is set on a terrace below the house, enclosed by tightly clipped hedges, and from the front of the house there are superb views of the sea.

cool minimalism

60 The jam factory

Warehouses, wharves, factories, tanneries, hospitals and schools all over London have been converted to residential use. Initially considered by many to be a passing fad, living in former manufacturing or industrial spaces has become a stylish and important alternative to traditional housing. Owners appreciate single-level living and the fact that they have a blank space on which to imprint their own style. In this case the term 'loft-living' is not used, as the owners clearly wanted to divide up the substantial space – realizing that a true open plan does not suit most people – but in a totally flexible way. They created two bedrooms by installing full-height, bi-fold sliding doors that virtually disappear when an open-plan layout is required. The second bedroom doubles as an office, enclosed only when guests are staying. To maximize daylight, the whole living area is open to a row of tall windows running the length of the apartment. Pure-white poured-resin floors are light, warm and practical, as is the white high-gloss finish on the kitchen units. Pure simplicity, pure pleasure.

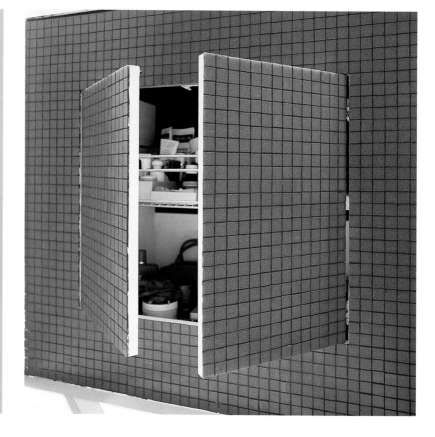

cool minimalism

61 Pure contrast

The contrast between the exterior of this three-hundred-year-old timber-framed German farmhouse and its pure-white interior could not be greater. Inserting steel supports on carefully arranged pillars opened up the ground-floor living areas. Between one pair of these pillars, the Düsseldorf-based interior designer arranged a gleaming white console to separate the spaces gently into a seating area, an open circulation space and dining area beyond. The white-tiled entrance-hall is deliberately masculine in feel, furnished with a French ebonized walnut console, a Chinese chair and a framed, very graphic piece of Bhuddist script written on palm leaves, hung above the table. Pure-white bedrooms and bathrooms feature chrome and marble detailing but there is absolutely no colour in the house apart from black and the natural tones of the wood floors and a collection of African animal sculptures. There was enough space within the roof area to build a wonderfully efficient dressing-room with a custom-made movable chest of drawers for storing belts and shoes, as well as enough cupboards to house a boutique.

cool minimalism

62 Riverside penthouse

Since the mid-1990s various parts of London have changed character completely as developers realize that former warehouses, industrial units and schools can be successfully converted into residential accommodation. Built on the New York model, loft living is now the choice of many who eschew traditional housing in favour of open-plan spaces, large windows and the chance to fit out an empty space in any style that takes their fancy. This large residential development in Southwark, south London, so impressed its builder–owner that he decided to take the penthouse for himself. Set high above the River Thames, with views in every direction, the apartment covers three floors, the bedrooms and bathrooms on the lower level, and the kitchen, living-room and study above. On the top of the building, reached via a spiral staircase, is the private roof-terrace. The whole is a slick space composed of stone, warm woods and glass, punctuated with a collection of contemporary art and sculpture, and the most fantastic views. The curved galley kitchen was designed by Piers Gough and includes two distinctive types of storage: plenty of open shelving for black and white china and glassware, plus a mix of under-counter cupboards and drawers. The seamless look is created by using the same timber for worktops and units.

63 Exemplary conversion

Contemporary interior design relies heavily on the twentieth-century avant-garde movements in architecture when function, technology and simplicity radically removed centuries of traditional building methods and decorative detailing. The style is all about asymmetrical composition, metal-and-glass construction, pure-white rendering and open-plan living. This is all very well when one is building from scratch, but here an architect and his wife, an interior designer, have turned an old dairy in the north of England into a lavish modern home. The dairy had first been converted into a home forty years ago, but nothing of that era was to remain. The design is notable for its use of cubes, glass bricks and grid-like windows, and the sheer simplicity of the interior fit-out. Oak and reclaimed Yorkstone floors provide the necessary change in texture and colour and the stainless-steel kitchen links perfectly to the couple's choice of dining furniture and open shelving. The glass-topped table is by Norman Foster and the metal chairs are a Charles Eames design. This house exemplifies current trends in contemporary style.

cool minimalism

64 Industrial space

Large former industrial buildings, stripped to bare brick and concrete, provide some of the most versatile spaces in which contemporary design and urban lifestyle have developed. The sheer lack of internal restriction and restraint, and the often-plentiful light, have driven designers to value the structural raw materials and to leave as much as possible exposed. The young owner–designer of this large raw space understood exactly how she wanted to mix brick and concrete walls with hardwood floors and plaster divisions, and keep the same natural tones for furnishings and decoration. She understood, too, that the size and scale of each item was critical in balancing such large open spaces. By leaving dividing walls short of the ceiling and keeping fittings boxy and substantial, she retained a strong sense of loft style but never neglected the need for certain barriers and division of function. The kitchen and Duktus maple bench and table set were supplied by Bulthaup and are low-key, functional and unobtrusive. Two large bedrooms with bathrooms and a terrace make this a rare city apartment.

cool minimalism

cool minimalism

65 Technical perfection

For a man who spends his days working in industrial design on a vast scale, it must have been an interesting exercise to put his mind to the relatively minor project that would become his office and home. The project was made possible by finding land on the outskirts of Hanover that would suit the business and his architectural vision of a live/work space. The steel-and-glass construction can be seen from miles away at night, when the fourth- and fifth-floor penthouse is lit up. There is a high degree of perfectionism and discipline in this house. The floors, for instance, are all of the same grey stone tiles, inside and out. There are no visible internal doors, just partitions of glass that slide into the walls. Even the roof-garden is planted in immaculate blocks of gentle colour. Walls are finished in polished marble stuccowork, which gleams and shines in contrast to the matt grey floors. Furniture includes modern classics from Le Corbusier, Spencer Fung, Eames and Christian Liaigre. Frank Gehry's cardboard chair stands at the foot of the bed.

cool minimalism

66   Urban renewal

When a couple, an architect and a building contractor, found an untouched apartment in a 1930s block in London, it was sure to become an original and exciting project. Unusually, it was set over two floors, was in a sought-after location and ripe for refurbishment. It was relatively easy to remove internal walls and get rid of the small rooms; even the concrete staircase, set into a narrow hall, was removed and replaced by a transparent glass-and-steel structure. Colour has been chosen with great care and is used in blocks on the walls and kitchen units, and even the pair of red sofas in a corner of the living-room continue the use of plain, strong colours as a statement. The apartment is very light, enhanced by the use of reflective surfaces, such as glass and highly polished stainless steel in the kitchen. The furnishings are a mix of designer names, Ikea and custom-made pieces. Upstairs it was possible to reconfigure the space to include an office, bedrooms and a sleek bathroom. Once again, mirrored glass helps to enlarge and light up enclosed spaces.

cool minimalism

country 67–90

67 Another country

Approached along a narrow country road, with a barren rocky ridge on one side and flat expansive farmland on the other, this grand bastide sits raised on a broad terrace, seemingly untouched for centuries. All is not what it seems, but so sensitive was the expert restoration of this range of Provençal barns that it is hard to imagine that this house was recently a ruin. The owners are American, the wife an interior designer who might have been an acolyte of Madame de Pompadour, such is her love of eighteenth-century French design and decoration. The architectural firm that carried out the work is renowned for their knowledge of period detail and ability to source the correct materials, be they fireplaces or window glass. While many of the rooms are filled with superb pieces from the period, this is a relaxed family home with numerous guest bedrooms, great entertaining spaces and intimate private quarters. Matt-grey and milky-white paintwork sets off collections of early Gien faïence, old oil paintings, Provençal fruitwood furniture and elaborate gilt frames. Many of the contents were bought locally, while fabrics came from Pierre Frey in Paris or from the United States. Highly detailed planning and the expertise of both owner and architect have created an exceptional family home, imbued with history and great presence.

country

68 Country classic

The English country house was, and still is, an important inspiration for many international designers, but there is nothing quite like the real thing. Formed of a central block built in 1680 and a 1720 extension of identical wings on either side, this ochre-washed brick house has barely changed since it was completed. Minor alterations were made to the interiors in the late twentieth century: the kitchen floor was raised, a warren of service rooms behind the rear staircase was opened up to become an informal sitting-room, and glass doors were added to the dining-room, giving access to a garden terrace. Several bedrooms became bathrooms, fitted out in period style with deep free-standing baths and plenty of large cupboards. The old wide-plank floors and staircases are original, and the decoration is pure country classic, relying on collections of textiles, antique furniture, mirrors, porcelain, and faded Oriental rugs, creating the impression of generations of occupation by the same family. The walls and panelling are painted in off-whites to balance the patterns, colours and textures of contemporary and antique textiles used for curtains and upholstery.

69 Dowager duchess

The old stone Dower House in north-east England was in urgent need of sympathy and restoration when the current owners came across it. Originally Elizabethan, it was rebuilt in 1801, but much of its character had been lost after generations of remodelling and partitioning. To create the perfect family home takes courage, talent and the knowledge that so much of the expenditure will be unseen, hidden in walls, roof-space and under floors, as the massive job of installing new plumbing and cabling is carried out. The designer–owner had done it all before, and fortunately all the furniture from the old house fitted perfectly. The ground-floor kitchen and dining-room had been a separate flat, and once it had been gutted, the owner went to Chalon in London for a new country-style kitchen to complement the large Aga cooker. The first-floor bedrooms and bathrooms are warm but pale. The expansive living areas on the ground floor are richer in detail and colour than those above, employing silks and suede, needlepoint and linen. The design is a triumph of function and country-house comfort.

70 Highland fling

Very few people actually buy castles, but this magnificent sixteenth-century colossus on the edge of the Firth of Moray in Scotland was found and restored by a man who, since childhood, had dreamed of owning and restoring such a place. Although bought as a ruin, it was nonetheless a late medieval Z-plan tower. Armed with little money but plenty of knowledge and lots of enthusiasm, the owners began a seven-year restoration programme. It was a labour of love: eighty-six windows and doors were made by local craftsmen; the correct timber, slate and stone had to be found; and, keen to avoid using any wrong materials, they mixed the lime and pigments for the exterior finish themselves. Fortunately, the owners' textile and carpet business manufactures designs with a Scottish history and palette, and they were able to use a great many of their own products throughout the interior. Some of the furniture was made at the castle and other pieces were inherited or bought locally. The walls are clad with either wooden planks or softly painted plaster, the windows are curtainless, but the beds and sofas are draped and warmed with hangings, blankets and woollen fabrics. An enormous challenge, this is a dream come true.

71 Village life

Near the Cabo de Creus, an hour's drive north of Barcelona, is the fishing village of Cadaques. The young couple who bought this old house were holidaying from France and decided it was the ideal place to return to. The most appealing aspect of the house was the way in which it was built into the hillside. It required no structural work, but all the services were renewed, and they were left with a blank canvas on which to add colour and texture. Grey, blue, green and yellow colour washes were applied, and previous layers of paint were scraped back to expose past colour-schemes in their mottled variations. As it is a summer holiday home furnishings were kept simple and inexpensive. Trestle tables, cotton ticking fabrics and market finds from all over Europe fit perfectly into the pretty, rustic interior. As there are no windows at the back of the house, it is cool and dimly lit – the perfect hot-weather retreat.

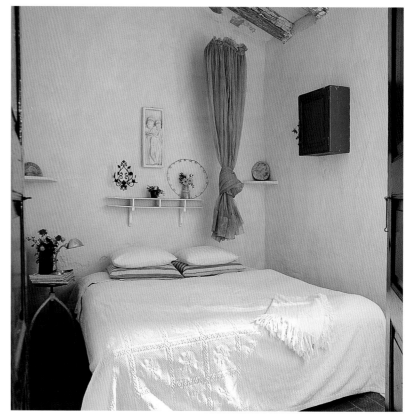

72 Summer hideaway

Major renovation or almost total rebuilding is sometimes required to bring a house up to date and back to life. With a principal residence in Switzerland, the owners of this house near Nice, in the South of France, had spent many happy holidays here but they decided it needed to be redesigned. A London-based design duo was asked to come up with plans. There were a number of problems associated with the 1930s stone building, and after much discussion it was agreed that the property would be rebuilt. It needed to be enlarged where possible, and a local architect–builder was called in to advise on construction and the supply of correct materials. In order to retain a strong country character, many of the stone walls were left in their natural state; others were just painted, while in some rooms they were both plastered and painted. Structural beams were exposed and the window frames left natural. Outdoor living is an essential part of any holiday home and in France it is usual to create several shady dining areas, but here cooler evenings have been catered for by building an open-sided pool-house, complete with fireplace. The interiors are furnished with a mix of contemporary and antique furniture and made cosy by the many warm-toned timbers used throughout the house.

73 Northern light

Set in rural East Anglia in the east of England, a group of three thatched cottages was converted into one dwelling by its Danish owner. The interiors of the house, and particularly the studio, reflect his love of all things Scandinavian, especially that luminous, soft grey-white that works so well in northern climates. He has not slavishly relied on Danish and Swedish pieces, but the overall impression is that of a country house in Sweden where French influences in the eighteenth and nineteenth centuries made quite an impact. The house and studio share the same calm and airy aesthetic, a monochrome world but one that is constantly changing with the seasons and varying levels of light. Floorboards, beams and panelled walls are all washed in the same colour; mirrors, chairs, a secrétaire and chest are similarly pale. There is little pattern to disturb the serenity – just a checked fabric used on a sofa and chairs, plain gunmetal grey here and there, and a floral stripe on a bedroom chair. Touches of silver, black and gilt punctuate the pale spaces, contrasting beautifully with the quiet grey wash.

74 Far pavilion

This gem of a miniature pavilion is one of a pair, set close to the stone boundary walls of a Provençal estate that includes a restored eighteenth-century hunting-lodge. Tiny but perfect in its proportions and detailing, it provides a quiet country retreat for a man who works in the frenetic world of international architecture and design. The pavilion contains few rooms – an entrance-hall, salon and conservatory-like kitchen on the ground floor, and two bedrooms and a bathroom on the first, both levels connected by a mahogany spiral staircase – but it nonetheless feels rather special. The setting is sublime and so is the classic French interior. The walls are completely covered in La Toile Villageoise of an old design in madder and cream, which has rapidly become antique in appearance from the open fire. Tall mirror-panelled cupboards are painted black, as is the specially made kitchen shelving. Black brings weight and balance to many interiors, effective here in the white-walled, glass-roofed kitchen. Apart from the piano, brought from the United States, all the contents are French, and most date from the eighteenth and nineteenth centuries, except the charming 1950s Jansen tole table with a tree-trunk base adorned with suitable wildlife.

75 Tuscan belle

Set four-square in the rich agricultural lands of eastern Tuscany, this eighteenth-century farmhouse has been restored by a Belgian artist and designer to become a multi-family holiday home. The house had been uninhabited for years and was almost derelict. A two-year restoration programme was undertaken in which careful preservation was the main objective. A loggia runs across the front, facing fields and a range of blue-green hills in the distance. The ground floor, formerly cattle barns, houses a large kitchen, a bedroom off the hallway and, down one side, an exotic 'Turquerie' that has been created with hand-painted fabrics and wall decorations. An enormous fireplace dominates the first floor, which would originally have been the kitchen. Now the room is used as a sitting-room, which is cool in summer and warm in winter. There are numerous bedrooms, each one differently but simply decorated in faded soft colours. All bathrooms are the same, varying only in shape and size. The designer and her architect worked in complete accord, one complementing the other, and at the project's completion nothing appears to be new and intervention seems minimal.

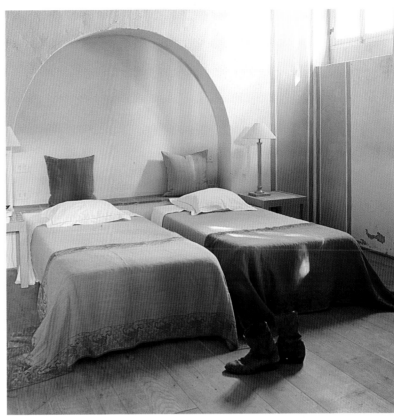

76 Perfect Provence

To many Parisians, and an international band of Francophiles, the Luberon and the area around St-Remy-de-Provence are some of the most coveted places in France in which to own a house. Apart from the climate, the views and the wonderful food and wine, there are first-class restorers, designers and craftsmen who can completely transform old farmhouses and manors to suit discriminating owners. This house is a superb example of a major architectural and design collaboration. Virtually everything was replaced, but with great sensitivity to proportion and period detail, and extensive use has been made of reclaimed materials – from floor-tiles and chimney-pieces to beams and doors. New stonework is supplied from quarries that have been in use for millennia. The interior decoration was carried out by a friend of the owners who owns a wonderful house near by, is well versed in French style and who knows the best sources for fabrics and furniture. Relying largely on white, cream and pale grey, she has created a cool and utterly restful interior of great comfort and style.

77 Crown jewel

An ancient house with royal connections and land has for centuries been something to which the English aspire. Often much reduced in size or, in the case of smaller houses, added to over the centuries, owners have to make numerous tough decisions about the future of such properties. This house bankrupted its builder in the sixteenth century, and later much of the enormous building was demolished. Even so, a sizeable portion remained, which was again extended in the 1800s. It has been owned by the same family ever since. The current family recognizes and enjoys the ups and downs of living in a historic house, including the fact that today such a house and garden have to pay their own way. Restoration is a constant consideration, with much of the investment going unseen into roof repairs or renewing electrical systems, but a great deal of the extraordinary charm of old houses lies in the many surviving layers of previous generations' pictures, furniture and fabrics. Bathrooms and kitchens have been updated but in an old-fashioned style, and while the house is a busy family home there is a palpable sense of history in every room. It takes great skill and energy to keep such a house so fresh and alive.

78 Chartreuse charm

Unusually, the garden of this fine and much-loved seventeenth- and eighteenth-century hunting-lodge in Périgord, south-west France, was laid out and replanted before the old internal partitions were stripped out to reveal the bones of the house. Unlike the garden, which is filled with roses and lush herbaceous planting, the house has a sparseness that its owner attributes, in part at least, to five years spent living in Japan. The walls are mostly a soft yellow, the floors are bare poplar boards, tiles or stone flags, and there are no curtains and few paintings. The walls are hung instead with groups of prints and drawings, some by Chardin and Henry Moore. Internal shutters control light, and even on a dull day the house glows with a gentle warmth. In the grand salon a pair of bookcases stand either side of the chimney-piece, and a Regency panel above it displays prints. Much of the French furniture is painted, and in the petit salon, red fabric from Mali covers the sofa while two Louis XVI chairs are in a fabric by Le Manach. English rush matting covers the floor. The bathrooms feature old-fashioned claw-foot baths and Pierre Frey fabric lining the cupboards. The chestnut beamed tower room, formerly a tobacco-drying barn, was opened up for use as a bedroom.

country

79 Cotswold country

The acquisition of a country house is often a tale of falling in love, not something that was difficult in this case, as the location in the Windrush Valley, a short distance from Oxford, is one of the most sought-after in England. The farmhouse, originally a pair of late fifteenth-century cottages, had been enlarged in all directions over the centuries. In the late 1990s it had settled as a rather tired Georgian creation, not without charm, but barely suited to its owner's international lifestyle and business. After a period of getting a feel for the house and its many outbuildings, she asked a local architect, a specialist in heritage work and the local vernacular, to advise on what would become a major transformation. Taking the seventeenth century and the Arts and Crafts movement as their base, they spent four years designing, altering and creating the manor house you can see today. One important factor was the fact that the house should age well. Lime plaster, sawn green oak and reclaimed flagstones immediately changed the interior, along with the sensitive removal of walls, allowing a better use of space. Small rooms and passages were swept away, windows enlarged or lowered, and a brand new bedroom wing was added. Opulent fabrics, Asian furniture and specially commissioned furniture combine to create an unusually stylish interior.

80 Modern Mallorca

Although Mallorca has become an increasingly busy tourist destination and favoured location for holiday homes, it takes only a step back from the coastline to realize that the island still has numerous old farmhouses for sale and some very special sites on which to build. A couple who once bought and restored a house here, originally as a holiday home, quickly made it their permanent base, and developed a thriving building, restoration and design business, catering to busy Europeans who need a reliable and knowledgeable team to create their own dream homes. The owner of this house was a client of theirs who favoured a new house in the country with plenty of shady seating areas, a pool and good-sized casual entertaining spaces, but the open site required a great deal of landscaping before building could begin. The use of architectural salvage and recycled materials plays an important part in the team's designs, providing new houses with a feeling of age and atmosphere. Furniture and fittings are from a wide range of sources, chosen for comfort or patina, shape or suitability. Both architect and designer have created a superb house with more than a nod to the vernacular, and it looks absolutely right in its dramatic island setting.

country

81 French leave

A charming nineteenth-century house in the Marne valley in France is where a well-known New Zealand artist lives and works, in a setting that is not so very different from her rural homeland. Admittedly, though, nobody in the Antipodes built houses like this – a charming bourgeois brick-and-stone mini château with numerous tall timber-framed windows screened by grey-blue painted shutters. Described as a ruin inside when bought, the interiors nonetheless still contained typical terracotta floor-tiles, old exposed beams and some cupboards, but within the restored shell a quirky mix of partitions has been added, designed to fulfil the owner's very specific requirements. Fitted within the formerly empty first floor is a plywood structure that divides the space into a bedroom, a sizeable library, a bathroom and an office. Much creative work has gone into enlivening the tired old rooms: paintings, of course, but also collections both decorative and unusual abound. The garden is a constant source of joy and produce, while the house provides an inspirational backdrop to artistic endeavour.

82 Coastal heritage

Everything about the interior of this house suits its remarkable location on England's Dorset coast, an area that was declared a World Heritage Site in 2002. The house, one of a pair, was built in the 1880s as a holiday home. The current owner, a designer, had dreamed of a seaside home for years and had rented cottages near by for some time but never expected she would find the right property as easily as she did. It had been a guesthouse for many years and required a formidable amount of work to upgrade the entire building. The former double garage became a very large kitchen/dining-room, designed to have the best possible views of the sea. The front-facing wall is entirely glass; the owner enclosed the large terrace across the façade but allowed for plenty of windows, one of which is framed by a weathered teak door frame. All the paintwork was bought or mixed to echo the colours of the local cliffs and fossils, and old pallets, driftwood and scaffolding have become shelves and cupboards. Although the scene is undoubtedly English, this interesting house has a colonial ambience about it that is relaxed, airy and supremely comfortable.

83 Entente cordiale

The owners of this estate near Le Mans in France have combined their possessions and style with great accord. The wife, an English interior designer, and her French husband took on the 1806 Directoire property immediately after their marriage. A pretty two-storey house with numerous guest bedrooms, some of which are set behind dormer windows in the roof, it has the classic, highly desirable proportions of the period. A broad, raised stone terrace graces the front, while in the centre is a double entrance-hall, the staircase rising from a smaller hall behind. To the left is a large reception room, and beyond it another, used for shooting parties, runs the full depth of the house. Reached by way of a bright corridor is the dining-room, and beyond that a large library, which links to the kitchen. The decoration throughout relies on a mix of wonderful antique furniture and English and French textiles. There is an old walled farmyard behind the house, and ponds, woods and fields surround the property, creating a private haven of peace and quiet.

84 Cornish cream

Located on the Cornish coast in south-west England, this 1960s house was turned into a much-loved family holiday home by the managing director of an international fabrics house. After replacing doors and removing all reminders of the 1960s, it seemed natural to follow both an American and an English tradition of using tongue-and-groove boarding and stripped and sanded floorboards as a starting point. Although traditional in feel, the use of pale colours, little pattern and functional furniture in simple shapes has established a classic summer look that is airy and light but warm in winter. A deep sofa and comfortable chairs in the main sitting-room are the only really large pieces. An antique chair, painted wooden chairs and cane chairs all look relaxed and casual, and blue has been effectively used, in stripes, checks and solid colour, as an appropriate seaside accent. Naturally the owner loves fabrics, and various linens and cottons have been used throughout the house. Curtains are casually looped up at the corners or left unlined to let in light and fresh air. The stairs have been painted in two tones to emulate a carpet runner but bare boards are the norm. Relaxed and friendly, this is an ideal holiday home.

85 Anglo-American

Warm climates demand architecture that allows a house and garden to be far more accessible to each other than is common in Northern Europe. Open verandas, perhaps slatted shutters to admit fresh air, and plenty of glazed doors are the norm, allowing the house to be opened up from back to front in the hot summer months. The interiors, though, can range from seaside resort to cosy country, and here an English owner asked a local designer to interpret an Anglo-American approach to a new house, set in idyllic surroundings on a lake in Georgia. It is a rich mix of antique, reproduction and contemporary furniture, textured fabrics, patterns and colour. Some corners of the house are definitely English in style; there is French country as well as American Federal furniture; and there are pieces of Oriental blue-and-white porcelain. Chairs and tables are set out on the wrap-around verandas, with the walls lined in white-painted clapboard. Tall trees set in trim green lawns shade parts of the house, and the views over the water are sensational.

86 Decorative sympathy

Acquiring a country house or cottage is an enduring and romantic dream for many people. A house in a forest, a converted barn or an old stable block – the setting and original purpose of the property doesn't seem to matter as long as it is in the countryside, but such a home is difficult to find in many countries. The owner of this two-hundred-year-old north German cottage is well aware of its rarity value. Found through word of mouth and previously owned by a couple who had the same decorative sympathies, little work was required to create exactly what the new owner wanted from her weekend and holiday retreat. The roof was re-thatched, a shower-room added and the whole place painted in the pale colours that reflect its location near the Danish border. Paint has transformed not only the interior but also most of the furniture: bought for shape and function, regardless of condition, it is all painted in the Scandinavian colours so beloved of its artistic châtelaine. This cottage has it all: a quiet agricultural location, sweeping views, a large pond and a garden that is developing into a cottage classic.

87 Georgian tradition

Set on rising ground within park-like gardens, this late Georgian house in mid-Wales was not in good repair when its owners first saw it, but the location, the views and the complete lack of neighbours convinced them that it could easily become a dream home. Architecture of this period is, of course, much sought-after. Room sizes and their number are usually good, often allowing generous en-suite bathrooms; window proportions have never been bettered; staircases are often top-lit; and, if luck would have it, a number of good marble fireplace surrounds will have survived. The owner is a London art dealer who specializes in British paintings, and his wife is an interior designer, so there was never any doubt that the refurbishment and decoration of their fairly large country house would be anything but a superb example of the genre. Naturally there are many wonderful works of art here, ranging from large equestrian canvases to small portraits. A warren of utility rooms became an adjoining kitchen and breakfast-room, French in style with doors leading to the garden. All the bedrooms are furnished in the best country-house tradition of gentle colour, comfort and warmth.

88 French polish

That rarefied part of Provence known as the 'Golden Triangle' (between Avignon, Arles and Aix-en-Provence) is filled with exceptionally beautiful homes, many with large, superbly designed gardens, of which this is a perfect example. Their owners come from Paris, Northern Europe, the United States and beyond. Rarely are the farmhouses, or 'mas' as they are known, in good enough condition to satisfy the desires of the new owners. Specialist firms in the region, with intimate knowledge of restoration techniques, now bring back to life many of the semi-ruined mas and bastides. Usually built of local limestone, they were originally the houses and barns that formed the hub of local farming communities, and the best restoration programmes make use of traditional methods and materials. Attached barns become drawing-rooms, tractor sheds make orangeries, and often a new staircase has to be built to reach the upper floors. So skilful is much of the work that it is barely possible to tell what is original and what is new. Window glass appears old, floor- and wall-tiles are reclaimed and carefully selected for patina, fireplace surrounds are bought second-hand from dealers, and walls are finished in traditional colours. It is a style that is much copied throughout the world but is never quite as good as the real thing.

89 Rescue and revival

It takes imagination and courage to turn a run-down group of Provençal buildings into a dream home, let alone find them in the first place, given the popularity of Provence as an international holiday destination where ownership is prized above renting. From the start the owner could visualize renovating this mid-1850s house, which is at the edge of a village, to fulfil her desire for open-plan summer and winter living. The kitchen and expansive ground-floor reception rooms were created by removing part of the existing stone dividing walls and inserting broad arches instead. Right across the front, French doors can be opened to blur the boundary between the inside and the full-width limestone terrace. The house contained some welcome secrets, revealed only after generations of plasterboard had been stripped out: wonderfully distressed beams, a grand fireplace and distinctive stonework indicated that the original builder was a man of some means. A major element of the works included building the interior of the barn, which now houses the master bedroom. The garden, formerly just a car park, has been transformed, and now at its centre is an enormous black swimming-pool, edged in stone and surrounded by fruit trees, roses, clematis and a wall of bamboo.

90 Traditional spirit

There are numerous difficult decisions to make during the restoration of
an old house. The balance between retaining the character and patina
of age, while bringing services and the flow of space up to date, can be
a daunting task, and the owners of this Mallorcan house called in a
respected designer to pull the project together. The house was a ruin
but, by taking great care to use local materials and finishes, they have
created a home of great charm that is suitable for both a modern
lifestyle and the sunny island setting. Floor finishes vary widely from
terracotta to pebble and tile. The interiors are relaxed, light and airy,
using shades of white, cream and soft blue and green; beams are
bleached or left in their natural wood tones. The furniture, most of
which is antique European, is either painted or waxed wood and the
choice of fabrics is summery and pale. Taking the view that they wanted
neither a town or country look the owners have mixed up the contents
in a relaxed manner, enlivening the pale scheme with touches of vivid
red, blue or black.

opulent 91–100

91 Period piece

Linking two or more apartments together has made possible the creation of several dream homes featured in this book. The Parisian, but London-based, owner of this very French interior was able to join two apartments and successfully ensure that he achieved the desired flow of space as well as the correct proportion and scale. The best rooms in the wonderful nineteenth-century stucco houses of London were the first-floor drawing- and dining-rooms, each with balconies, which in this case overlook a garden square. After removing countless flimsy partitions, the original proportions were revealed in all their glory. As a dealer in Empire and Regency furniture, and a design and decoration consultant, the owner has created a fine set of rooms, choosing the best examples of craftsmanship spanning a century or so. The three major rooms are the salon, library and bedroom, the last of these leading to a pair of en-suite bathrooms and custom-made dressing-rooms. Everything about this superb apartment illustrates its owner's knowledge and skill, his mastery of colour and drama, and his desire to leave the twenty-first century outside his door.

92 Treasure trove

The homes of antiques dealers tend to imitate their shops or a stand at a fair and this south London house is no exception. The owners, who dislike polite, safe furniture, live in an exotic and eccentric setting, filled with plunder from all over the world. One could say that this is less about design and more about haphazard display, but a closer look reveals that order and artistic flair govern the arrangement of this ever-changing collection. Prints and pictures are crammed onto walls from floor to ceiling, cabinets of every style and shape are filled with objets d'art spanning several centuries, and nearly everything has an intriguing story. Condition is less important than the human connection; provenance is what fascinates these dealers, and relics are sought out in salerooms and markets all over Europe. Busts, buffalo skulls, a Communist hoarding from the Berlin wall, stuffed animals, ancient brocades and rivets from the Eiffel Tower are just a sample of what is to be seen. The most opulent room, Turkish in style, is a *tour-de-force* of an adventurer's dream come true.

93 Rescue and revival

Rarely, in the last decade, have paint effects been used in a domestic interior in a manner so wonderfully over-the-top as in this east London house. Standing huddled together on a busy road, a small group of early eighteenth-century town houses has survived bombing, demolition and every ravage known to urban regeneration, to shine as fine examples of one of the greatest periods of British architecture. When the owner, a designer and expert on paint finishes, first saw the house it was largely open to the sky with little to recommend it but for some original wall-panelling. This, of course, was an opportunity to rebuild and revive a historic survivor in a highly personal manner, but also in a way that decoratively acknowledged its past centuries. Following the same room layouts as the original, it was just a matter of choosing favourite fantastic devices from the Italian Renaissance to 1940s Paris with which to decorate every single surface. There are *trompe l'oeil* figures and columns, what appear to be antique plastered walls, old stamped-leather panels, French Empire motifs, and cloud-like painted skies, no longer blue but fogged and smoked as if original to the house. The imagination and sheer quality of the work should be applauded and cherished.

94 High drama

Belgravia, in central London, is filled with grand stuccoed terraces of tall sober houses, many of which have been used as embassies or ambassadorial residences for years. Others, though, provide magnificent spaces for the most exuberant of owners to fulfil their fantasies. This house is richly coloured, the use of velvet for upholstery and the brilliant tones of gilt picture-frames and mirrors creating a lavish ensemble. The antique fireplaces are French and bold, curtains are full and rich, and the furniture is a wonderful mix of traditional shapes dressed up in exotic style, reminiscent of a Venetian interior. The use of intense colour is not only confined to the reception rooms; bedrooms and bathrooms also fizz with colour and the shimmer of silk. The kitchen and dining-room have touches of Gothic, and the owner prefers to commission unusual pieces from a wide circle of artistic friends rather than buy more conventionally. To achieve a paint finish such as the blue on the walls of the dining-room requires a skilled practitioner who is prepared to work with several tones in layers, creating a depth of colour and a finish far richer than flat paint can ever achieve. A dream home is essentially one without restraint of any kind.

opulent

95 Vibrant background

Balance and proportion are the tenets by which this London-based interior designer approaches his work. His own home, on the top two floors of an 1875 Dutch-style house in south London, illustrates this belief as well as his innovative ideas and bold sense of colour. Using standard Sanderson paints he created a vibrant background for an interesting collection of furniture, ranging from the bright-red 1960s Pierre Paulin chairs in the living-room to his own-design glass-and-steel kitchen table and circular side-tables. He also designed an unusual system to screen the living-room window: four plywood forms, rather like aircraft wings, are covered in four toning silk fabrics and hung from a track above the window. They can be twisted to give complete control of the light source. Instead of just painting the kitchen cupboards, the owner bonded a dark-blue leather cloth on to the doors and used tambour shutters above the worktop to hide clutter. Conscious of texture as well as colour, he chose stainless-steel floor-tiles, originally made for Charles de Gaulle airport in Paris.

opulent

96 Colour conscious

For many people, period architecture with original interior detailing is the ultimate way to live. One of Hamburg's foremost interior designers was asked by a friend to assess a 1906 Jugenstil apartment, set beside an Alster canal, and agreed that it was a rare gem. The doors, floors and windows were original, and unusually the layout works as well today as it did a century ago. The entrance leads to a wide corridor, off which all the rooms are accessed. Tall French doors overlooking balconies and the tree-lined street beyond light a pair of reception rooms to the right. A series of good-sized walk-in cupboards along one side of the hall have been adapted as areas for laundry and storage, and the largest is now a bathroom. Opposite is the main bedroom, exuberantly lined in red-and-white toile. Both owner and designer are passionate about colour, favouring intense eighteenth- and nineteenth-century pigments and papers over contemporary neutrals. It would be difficult to decorate in this manner if the apartment did not contain so many old-fashioned elements, in particular the tall doorways and luxurious ceiling heights.

97 Sense of purpose

A deep, distressed Pompeiian red begins at the entrance of this London house and goes all the way up the staircase, setting the scene for a home that was designed for the owners and their very special collection of Roman sculpture. The rather complicated red-brick Chelsea house was originally designed as a home and studio, which suited the new incumbents, both of whom are collectors and dealers. The collaboration of owner and interior designer produced an extremely individual environment in which the collection takes precedence over the more usual domestic comforts. The studio spaces on the ground and top floor are high-ceilinged and airy, and were designed as simple backdrops for the massive carvings they hold. The living spaces provided more of a challenge but by reworking the cornices and woodwork and creating a living-room-cum-library on the first floor, the small rooms took on a more important air. As well as designing two staircases, cornicing and French panelling, the designer also made furniture: a pair of stools in the manner of Thomas Hope, simple side-tables and a pair of bookcases in white and gilt were added to a collection of seventeenth- and eighteenth-century English and Italian furniture.

98 English heritage

Brighton, on England's south coast, is best known for its extraordinary Pavilion, but the town's wealth of Regency architecture comes a close second. Throughout the twentieth century, houses in the grand terraces and squares were constantly divided into smaller spaces, so the chance to buy an entire house, albeit one used as student accommodation for most of the century, was an exceptional opportunity. The sheer scale of the rooms is spectacular: the basement is vast, and the staircase of palatial proportions. Extraordinarily, many of the intricate mirror frames, pelmets and mouldings were intact, white gloss paint covering the original gilt. Each floor comprises a connected double space, with extensive curved glass windows front and back. The ground floor houses a contemporary kitchen and dining-room. The first floor contains a reception room, its other half used for musical evenings. A master suite of bedroom, bathroom and Oriental drawing-room fills the second floor. There are nine bedrooms in all, a media room, swimming-pool and gardens, and spectacular views of the beach.

99 Perfect Paris

The great *hôtels particulier* (private mansions) of Paris provide some of the city's most spectacular apartments. Here, in the Marais and set on the first floor of a 1620s rose-pink brick house near the Place des Voges, is a magnificent gem belonging to a well-known decorator. The building, which was used as offices for many years, is now divided into four apartments: the first floor, which has the largest rooms and the highest ceilings, has long been the most coveted. A great deal of work had to be carried out as part of the building's restoration, but some original panelling survived, to be stripped of paint and then waxed. Floors, doors and stairs were found to suit the architecture and the owner's predilection for correct period detail. While the impression is one of grandeur, the apartment relies on simple fabrics and furniture and high-quality craftsmanship to create the style. The owner's daughter made the over-scaled plaster atlantes (Atlas figures) either side of the fireplace in the main salon. This grand gesture is balanced by simple twentieth-century furniture and white cotton canvas. In an apartment of this size, one's dreams need no restraint.

100 Period panache

The great thing about being an interior designer with a shop full of beautiful fabrics and furniture, and a range of paints of one's own choosing, is the speed at which a home can be transformed. Designers famously try out furniture, colours, pictures, chandeliers and fabrics at home; sometimes they are sold on, sometimes they stay for years, but being able to experiment without fear of disapproval is one of the joys of the business. The German owner of this 1920s apartment uses it as an extension of his shop and is greatly taken with the atmosphere of the building, where all his neighbours are owner-occupiers. Creating the perfect home is as much about colour and design as it is about environment and atmosphere. There are many European influences at work here, from France, Scandinavia and England. The walls are painted in rich colours but are not cluttered with pictures. Scale is important and large mirrors are a favourite device to reflect light and add depth to the rooms. Antique fabrics are considered essential to tone down newly decorated rooms and imbue them with a sense of past life and history.

Credits

1 Owner: Jasper Conran.

2 Owners: Rory and Elizabeth Brooks. Architect: David Barrable at Sproson Barrable Ltd. Art: (clockwise from top far left) first page, picture 1: work on left-hand wall by Bridget Riley; picture 2: work hanging in centre by Alison Lambert; picture 3: work seen behind table by Howard Hodgkin; picture 7: work seen above stairs by William Turnbull, work seen below stairs by Patrick Heron; second page, picture 1: painting seen in mirror by Sara Rossberg; picture 5: work above fireplace by Ivon Hitchens.

3 Owner: Kelly Hoppen. Interior design: Kelly Hoppen Interiors.

4 Interior design: Wessel Freytag von Loringhoven.

5 Owner/interior designer: Charlotte Crosland, Charlotte Crosland Interiors. Feature originally sourced and produced by Amanda Harling.

6 Owner: Clare and Mark Hanson. Design: Hanson Interiors.

7 Architect: Hudson Featherstone (now working separately as Hudson Architects and Featherstone Associates).

8 Interior design: Candy and Candy, London.

9 Interior design: Cheryl Tague, Tague Design Associates.

10 Architect: John Simpson. Feature originally sourced and produced by Amanda Harling.

11 Interior design: David Collins Studio.

12 Owners: Fiona and David Mellor. Designer: David Mellor.

13 Todhunter Earle Interiors www.todhunterearle.com.

15 Interior design: Constanze von Unruh, Constanze Interior Projects Ltd. Feature produced by Amanda Harling.

16 Owner: John and Julie Gibson Jarvie.

Furnishings and accessories from Atelier, London SW11, UK, tel: +44 (0)20 7978 7733, email: info@atelierliving.com. Feature originally sourced and produced by Pattie Barron.

17 Interior design: Julia Korzilius Fine Interiors. Feature originally sourced and produced by Victoria Ahmadi.

18 Owner/interior designer: Frank Faulkner. Feature originally sourced and produced by Victoria Ahmadi.

19 Architect/interior designer: Nico Rensch, www.architeam.co.uk.

20 Design by Dorte Wehmeyer, An Den Kastanien, 1, 50859 Cologne, Germany, tel: +49 221 500 2204. Feature originally sourced and produced by Amanda Harling.

21 Architect: Peter Wadley Architects. Interior design: Fleur Rossdale, The Interior Design House. Feature originally sourced and produced by Amanda Harling.

22 Owner/interior designer: Lesley Cooke. Architect: Jason Cooper.

23 Interior designer: Reed/Boyd (now working separately as Studio Reed and Ann Boyd Ltd).

24 Interior design: Jane Whitfield.

25 Interior design: Janet Chisholm and Michael Sofaer. Feature originally sourced and produced by Nerida Piggin.

26 Architect/interior designer: Reinhard Weiss, 3s Architects LLP.

27 Design: Candy and Candy, London.

28 Interior design: Nina Campbell. Photography by Andreas von Einsiedel, courtesy of *House and Garden* (UK).

29 Interior design: Philip Hooper, Colefax & Fowler. Feature originally sourced and produced by Pattie Barron.

30 Design: Chester Jones, 240 Battersea Park Road, London SW1 4NG, UK, tel.: +44 (0)20 7498 2717.

31 krohleder@rohleder.com, www.rohleder.com.

32 Interior design: Rolf Sachs. Art: (clockwise from top far left) picture 1: works either side of the arch by Rolf Sachs; picture 2: work on the wall to the left by George Condo, work on the wall between the door and the shelves by Luis Leo; picture 3: work above fireplace by Eugene Leroy, work to left of arch by Georg Baselitz, works to right of arch and on right-hand wall by Arnulf Rainer; second page, picture 1: work hung on wall by Francesco Clemente; picture 2: work above fireplace by Walter Dahn, sculpture on left of mantelpiece by Cesar, work seen through arch in the next room by Eugene Leroy. Feature originally sourced and produced by Susanne von Meiss.

33 Interior design: Homeira Pour Heidari. Art: top left: by Richard Caldicott.

34 Interior design: Sheila Harley.

35 Interior design: Looby Crean Ltd. Feature originally sourced and produced by Pattie Barron.

36 Feature originally sourced and produced by Heidede Carstensen.

37 Interior design: Filippa Naess. Feature originally sourced and produced by Pattie Barron.

38 Interior design: Kelly Hoppen.

39 Interior design: Bruno Raymond, Ibiza, www.lamaisondelelephant.com. Feature originally sourced and produced by Sabine Wesemann.

40 Design: Chester Jones, 240 Battersea Park Road, London SW1 4NG, UK, tel.: +44 (0)20 7498 2717. Pictures courtesy of EWA Associates.

41 Interior design: Annabel Astor.

42 Interior design: Stephanie Hoppen. Feature originally sourced and produced by Amanda Harling.

43 Owner: Mr and Mrs Pieter van Naeltwijck. Architect: Alexandre Lafourcade, at Bruno et Alexandre

Lafourcade, 10 Boulevard Victor Hugo, 13210 Saint Remy-de-Provence, France, tel.: +33 490 92 10 14.

44 Interior design: Sarah Stewart Orecchia.

45 Interior design: Carolinda Tolstoy, www.carolinda-tolstoy.co.uk.

46 Design: Nick Etherington-Smith.

47 Design: Marc Johnson. Feature originally sourced and produced by Amanda Harling.

48 Interior design: Toni Muntaner, Mallorca. Feature originally sourced and produced by Amanda Harling.

49 Owned and designed by Carol and Ian Gordon.

50 Feature originally sourced and produced by Amanda Harling; subsequent feature produced by Sally Griffiths.

51 Steven Harris Architects, New York.

52 Interior design; Toni Muntaner, Mallorca. Feature originally sourced and produced by Amanda Harling.

53 Design: Mary Rose Young, Ceramicist. Feature originally sourced and produced by Heidede Carstensen. Pictures courtesy of EWA Associates.

54 Owner/designer: Hannes Myburgh, Meerlust Estate, Stellenbosch, South Africa.

55 Architect: Wolf Siegfried Wagner. Interior design: Nona von Haeften. Feature originally sourced and produced by Amanda Harling.

56 Architect: Hugh Newell Jacobsen, FAIA.

57 Feature originally sourced and produced by Pattie Barron.

58 Owner: Ranjit Murugason. Architect: Ferhan Azman, Azman Associates, 18 Charlotte Road, London EC2A 3PB, UK.

59 Architect/interior designer: Bataille-Ibens, Antwerp.

60 Owners: Simon Dobson (Simon

Dobson Construction, tel.: +44 (0)7939 048770) and Sarah Paskell. Architect: David Miller, tel.: +44 (0)20 7636 3120. Art: (top left and far left) work by Felice Hodges.

61 Interior design: Wessel Freytag von Loringhoven.

62 Architect and design: Manhattan Loft Corporation.

63 Design: Chris and Joanne Pearson, email: jo@ashleydesigncon.co.uk. Feature originally sourced and produced by Amanda Harling.

64 Interior design: Tara Bernerd. Pictures courtesy of Redcover Ltd.

65 Architect/Designer: Bernd Künne. Feature originally sourced and produced by Sabine Wesemann.

66 Interior design Gordana Mandic Buro, Buro Design, London, tel.: +44 (0)20 7351 3107. Feature originally sourced and produced by Amanda Harling.

67 Owner and designer: Ginny Magher of Ginny Magher Interiors, Atlanta. Architectural restoration: Bruno et Alexandre Lafourcade, 10 Boulevard Victor Hugo, 13210 Saint Remy-de-Provence, France, tel.: +33 490 92 10 14.

68 Architect (alterations): Christopher Smallwood.

69 Interior design: Annie Constantine.

70 Architecture and design: Lachlan and Annie Stewart of ANTA.

71 Design: Anders and Tami Christiansen. Feature originally sourced by Sally Griffiths. Pictures courtesy of Redcover Ltd.

72 Architecture/design: Collett-Zarzycki Ltd in association with Robert Dallas. Feature originally sourced and produced by Heidede Carstensen.

73 Designer: Jorn Langberg. Feature originally sourced and produced by Sally Griffiths. Pictures courtesy of Redcover Ltd.

74 Architecture and design: Kenyon Kramer/Jean-Louis Raynaud Associates, 3 Place des 3 Ormeaux, 13100 Aix-en-Provence, tel.: +33 4 42 23 52 32.

75 Interior design: Isabelle de Borchgrave. Architect: Jean-Philippe Gauvin.

76 Architect: Alexandre Lafourcade at Bruno et Alexandre Lafourcade, 10 Boulevard Victor Hugo, 13210 Saint Remy-de-Provence, France, tel.: +33 490 92 10 14. Interior design: Ginny Magher Interiors, Atlanta.

77 Interior design consultant: Anne Millais. Feature originally sourced and produced by Amanda Harling.

78 Owner and designer: Monsieur Antonin.

79 Interior design: Alison Henry at Alison Henry Ltd. info@alisonhenry.com.

80 Architect: Wolf Siegfried Wagner. Interior design: Nona von Haeften. Feature originally sourced and produced by Amanda Harling.

81 Design: Julia Morison.

82 Interior design: Juliet de Valero Wills at Design Dorset.

83 Interior design: Sophie Stonor-von Hirsch.

84 Interior design: Anne Grafton. Feature originally sourced and produced by Pattie Barron.

85 Interior design: Joan Brendle. Feature originally produced by Amanda Harling.

86 Interior design: Monique Waqué, tel.: +49 173 240 52 53.

87 Interior design: Penny Morrison of Morrison Interiors, tel.: +44 (0) 1547 560 460, bazzamor@aol.com.

88 Architecture and restoration: Bruno et Alexandre Lafourcade, 10 Boulevard Victor Hugo, 13210 Saint Remy-de-Provence, France, tel.: +33 490 92 10 14.

89 Interior Design by Sally Jeeves.

90 Interior: Holger Stewen Interior Design. Architecture: Fritz Hauri.

Feature originally sourced and produced by Victoria Ahmadi.

91 Interior design: André de Cacqueray, Adec Ltd, 227 Ebury Street, London SW1W 8LT, UK, tel.: +44 (0)20 7730 5000, e-mail: cacqueray@adecdesign.com. Feature originally sourced and produced by Sally Griffiths. Pictures courtesy of Redcover Ltd.

92 Interior design: Fiona and Warner Dailey.

93 Interior design: David Carter, tel.: +44 (0)20 7790 0259, mobile: +44 (0)7973 653944, e-mail: david@alacarter.com, www.alacarter.com.

94 Interior design: Amanda Eliasch. Art: picture top left, painting above fireplace by Theo Platt.

95 Architectural designer: Charles Rutherfoord. Feature originally sourced and produced by Amanda Harling.

96 Interior design: Peter Nolden, Peter Interior Design, www.peter-interior-design.de/www.peter-interior-farben.de.

97 Interior design: Chester Jones, 240 Battersea Park Road, London SW11 4NG, UK, tel.: +44 (0)20 7498 2717. Client: Ingrid McAlpine. Pictures courtesy of EWA Associates.

98 Interior design: Charles Style, Angel Property, tel.: +44 (0)20 8871 2666.

99 Architecture/Interior designer: Patrice Nourissat. Feature originally sourced and produced by Sally Griffiths. Pictures courtesy of Redcover Ltd.

100 Interior design: Peter Nolden, Peter Interior Design, www.peter-interior-design.de / www.peter-interior-farben.de. Feature originally sourced and produced by Victoria Ahmadi.

Acknowledgements

Andreas von Einsiedel would like to thank warmly the many owners, designers and architects featured in this book.

First published 2005 by Merrell Publishers Limited

Head office
81 Southwark Street
London SE1 0HX

New York office
740 Broadway, Suite 1202
New York, NY 10003

merrellpublishers.com

British Library Cataloguing-in-Publication Data:
Einsiedel, Andreas
Dream Homes : 100 inspirational interiors
1.Interior decoration
I.Title II.Thornycroft, Johanna
747

ISBN-13: 978-1-8589-4297-1
ISBN-10: 1-8589-4297-7

Produced by Merrell Publishers
Designed by Martin Lovelock
Copy-edited by Helen Miles
Proof-read by Kim Richardson
Printed and bound in China